Living I

Living In the World Of

Tyranny

Abiyah Israel

ACKNOWLEDGEMENTS

First and foremost, I would like to thank the creator of heaven and earth the Most High God for bestowing his blessings upon me. Without God nothing is possible. Also, I would like to thank my wife and my children for continual support through the trials of life. I would like to give a thank you to all my family and friends who kept me in their prayers throughout this entire process. I would also like to extend my heartfelt gratitude to all the supporters of We the People University, who have consistently backed the channel without fail. Your support means the world to us. Thank you, everyone, sincerely.

Living In the World of Tyranny

Table of Contents

1	Why I Became A Cop	4
2	The Academy Experience	12
3	Questioning The Training	20
4	Field Training	25
5	My Interactions	48
6	Traffic Stops	62
7	The Hypocrisy	71
8	The Mind of Cops	80
9	The Beginning of the End	85
10	The Downfall	97
11	Looking Good for the Camera	107
12	What's Next	109

Shout Out to Now Captain Ed..................114
When Dealing with Cops...........................116
Search & Seizure...118
Auditing Tips...126
About the Author.......................................132

Chapter 1

Why I Became a Cop:

I chose a career in law enforcement for several reasons. Firstly, I was in need of a job to support myself. Secondly, I wanted a profession where I could make a meaningful impact by helping others. And thirdly, I yearned for a role that allowed me a sense of freedom; the idea of being tied to a desk for eight or ten hours a day was something I couldn't tolerate. I always felt confined when stuck in one place, unlike my wife, who thrived in a desk job.

The initial hurdle I faced in pursuing a law enforcement career was my wife's concern and apprehension. She was understandably worried about the risks involved. To address her concerns, I decided to take a different route initially and became a paramedic. Working in the field of public service alongside law enforcement, I hoped this would alleviate some of her fears.

After gaining valuable experience as a paramedic, I transitioned to working inside the county jail, where I spent nearly three years honing my skills and gaining insights into the criminal justice system.

I believe that working within a county jail offers invaluable training for aspiring law enforcement officers and should be considered a mandatory requirement for all. The rationale behind this assertion is multifaceted: within the confines of a jail, officers do not have access to firearms, tasers, or batons, which necessitates a unique skill set. In the jail I served in, only supervisors possessed tasers; all other deputies had to learn how to deescalate chaotic situation without any extra equipment.

This environment demanded the acquisition of adept de-escalation skills. Those lacking proficiency in de-escalation techniques faced significant challenges in their roles as deputies. The significance of this training becomes evident when transitioning to a role as a police officer patrolling the streets, armed with lethal and non-lethal weaponry, such as guns, tasers, and solid metal batons. The presence of these tools without adequate de-escalation skills can lead to a concerning tendency to resort to force at the slightest hint of trouble.

When we talk about "de-escalation skills," we're referring to a set of techniques and communication strategies that law enforcement officers should use to defuse tense or potentially violent situations without resorting to force. These skills are essential for several reasons:

1. **Preservation of Life:** The primary goal of law enforcement is to protect and serve the community. De-escalation skills help officers minimize the risk of using lethal force, which can save lives, including the lives of the individuals they are dealing with and their own.

2. **Reduction of Use of Force Complaints:** When officers effectively de-escalate situations, it often results in fewer complaints of excessive force from the public. This helps build trust between law enforcement and the community they serve.

3. **Legal and Ethical Considerations:** The use of force by law enforcement is subject to legal and ethical standards. Officers must use force only when it's necessary and proportional to the threat. De-escalation techniques are a crucial part of ensuring that the use of force is justifiable under these standards.

4. **Conflict Resolution:** De-escalation skills not only help in diffusing immediate threats but also in resolving conflicts and disputes more peacefully. This contributes to the overall safety and well-being of the community.

Now, let's address the scenario that I mentioned in my original statement, where a deputy or police officer has access to various weapons like guns, tasers, batons, and OC spray but lacks de-escalation skills. This situation is concerning for several reasons:

- **Increased Risk of Escalation:** Without de-escalation skills, an officer is more likely to resort to using weapons when confronted with a potentially confrontational situation. This escalation can quickly turn a manageable situation into a dangerous one.

- **Negative Community Perception:** The use of force without apparent justification can erode public trust in law enforcement. Communities expect officers to employ their authority responsibly and to prioritize non-violent solutions whenever possible.

- **Legal Consequences:** Although we know in most cases cops will police themselves and nothing happens when they cross the line, but for the sake of making the point I'll continue to explain how things are supposed to work. An officer who consistently defaults to forceful responses without attempting de-escalation may find themselves facing legal consequences if their actions are deemed excessive or unjustified.

De-escalation skills are not just a desirable attribute for law enforcement officers; they are a fundamental requirement. These skills promote safer interactions between officers and the public, reduce the use of force, and ultimately contribute to a more just and secure society. Therefore, individuals aspiring to be deputies or police officers must undergo training and continuously develop their de-escalation skills to effectively fulfill their roles and responsibilities.

Another compelling reason why it's crucial to gain experience working inside a jail before transitioning to street duty as a police officer is that working in a jail environment exposes and challenges one's fears. For individuals who harbor apprehensions about various aspects of law enforcement, particularly those who tend to fear everything, the jail setting can be particularly demanding.

For instance, I want to address my own experience which involved working in an open bay area within a jail. An open bay setup does not have individual cells for inmates but rather a large, open space accommodating a maximum of

72 inmates with only one deputy present. In such an environment, if you carry a significant amount of fear within you, it becomes apparent not only to yourself but to the inmates as well.

In my experience, two common outcomes emerged for individuals with excessive fear in this situation. First, some deputies were so overwhelmed by fear that they either resigned from their position or requested a different assignment, because they were unable to perform their duties effectively in an open bay area. Second, there were those who chose to confront their fears and adapt, learning how to de-escalate tense situations and effectively manage the challenges presented to them.

The latter group of jail deputies, who overcame their fears and developed the necessary skills, were the ones well-prepared to transition to street duty. They did so without being burdened by an irrational fear of every little thing or an unfounded belief that everyone they encountered in public had a malicious intent. It's essential to emphasize that officers whose fears dictate their actions can inadvertently harm others, as their fear-driven responses may lead to unnecessary confrontations and escalations.

Experiencing the jail environment offers valuable insight into one's capacity to manage fear and develop crucial de-escalation skills. Those officers who successfully address their fears are better equipped to serve on the streets without allowing unwarranted apprehension to drive their actions, ultimately contributing to safer and more effective law enforcement.

Living In the World of Tyranny

After transitioning from the jail environment, I became a law enforcement officer patrolling the streets. But before I speak further on that I'd like to provide another example to illustrate why I believe it's essential to gain experience in a jail before serving as a cop on the street. There are tons of valuable lessons one can learn by beginning their law enforcement career inside a jail.

I recall a specific training scenario during my time working in a jail located on the west coast of Florida. This particular training took place in a dedicated area within the facility. This area was a section of the jail that was devoid of inmates and reserved solely for training purposes. During this exercise, our field training officers, also known as training deputies, would dress up as inmates. They would then select a group of three or four rookie deputies, me included, and take us into this training area.

Inside this designated space, they would orchestrate a deliberately chaotic scene, mimicking a situation that requires strong de-escalation skills. Despite being aware that the "inmates" were actually fellow deputies participating in a training exercise, it was surprisingly easy to immerse ourselves in the scenario. The realism was striking. Upon entering the open bay, the training deputies would simulate a tumultuous environment, complete with the deafening noise of 72 people shouting at the top of their lungs. The objective was to recreate a situation resembling a recent fight or an ongoing altercation.

Before I go on, please allow me to provide a brief description of myself and my partner at the time to help you understand the significance of this training. I stand at six feet four inches tall and weigh 240 pounds, while my partner measures six feet five inches in height and weighs 260 pounds.

While my partner and I were not the largest individuals, we certainly weren't small either. As we entered the open bay, we approached one of the deputies who was acting as an inmate. In this training exercise, this particular deputy was a woman, and she wasn't complying with our commands. We quickly took her to the ground, and her hands were tucked beneath her body, making it challenging to get her to comply. We continued to shout, "Stop resisting! Stop resisting! Give us your hands!" while she repeatedly replied, "I can't."

Despite hearing her protests, we insisted that she comply, demanding she give us her hands. We began to mimic striking maneuvers and simulate the application of pressure points as part of the training to make her comply so that we could handcuff her. Once the exercise was over, she approached us and imparted a life-changing lesson.

She asked us about our height, and we replied with our respective heights, 6'4" and 6'5". Then she inquired about our weights. After we shared our weights, she pointed out that we were significantly taller and heavier than she was. She emphasized that when her hands were pinned beneath her, she genuinely couldn't give us her hands due to the weight of our bodies pressing down on her. She made it clear that, in this situation, we had employed unnecessary uses force by mimicking strikes maneuvers and simulating pressure points due to us giving her orders that she physically could not follow. When she explained the situation to us, in an effort to teach us how to be better deputies, she did so calmly and politely.

Even though this was just a training exercise, her explanation hit me hard, and I felt a sincere sense of remorse. It made me reflect on the possibility of applying such force to a real-life citizen. What if I issued commands that were impossible for a person to obey and then punished them for not following those orders? This lesson stayed with me for a long time, a reminder that as police officers, we must be mindful of the commands we give, the clarity of those commands, and the potential consequences if they cannot be followed.

As police officers, we can become so engrossed in the intensity of the moment that we fail to grasp the difficulty or impossibility of the orders we issue. It's crucial to assess each situation carefully and make informed decisions, because if we overlook this responsibility it can result in harm to innocent people. This is one of the key reasons I advocate for police officers to work in a jail first, to learn de-escalation skills before patrolling the streets and carrying a collection of weapons. It's a lesson I will never forget.

After my tenure in the jail, I transitioned to serving on the street as a police officer, and this marked the true beginning of my journey, particularly my experience at the police academy.

Chapter 2

The Academy Experience

Prior to commencing my journey at the Academy, I had to undergo the rigorous hiring process. This process was quite lengthy in nature; therefore, it will lead one to believe that police departments are diligently searching for the most qualified individuals to join their ranks. However, this assumption doesn't hold true. They meticulously scrutinize your background, delving into all aspects, regardless of how distant they may be in your past, and pose deeply unsettling questions. Initially, I couldn't fathom the rationale behind the questions that they asked. Over time, I came to realize that some rather weird individuals had found their way onto the police force. Therefore, I convinced myself this was the reasoning for the questions.

One question they asked during the interview process was: "Have you ever been in trouble involving children?" This question left me perplexed and offended. It seemed like an unusual and insulting inquiry. Not only did they pose such unsettling questions, but they also conducted neighborhood surveys, asking my neighbors similar questions under the guise of gauging my character. They reached out to my family, interviewed my friends, and delved into every conceivable topic, not leaving any room for anything to fall through the cracks. Despite my initial belief that they were searching for the most qualified candidates, I was becoming very uncomfortable with their line of questions, but I went along with it, continuing to convince myself that they were seeking the best person to become a police officer in their department.

Another phase of the hiring process was completing a demanding fitness test. This was a test that I had to truly prepare my body for. It proved to be quite challenging, but I dedicated myself to rigorous training and ultimately passed. However, I couldn't help but notice that some individuals who hadn't trained as diligently still secured positions. It became evident that their connections within the department played a pivotal role in their hiring. This realization completely reversed my belief that merit, and qualifications were the primary criteria for employment; instead, it seemed that knowing someone within the department, be it a relative like a parent, aunt, or uncle, was the key to getting hired.

When I finally received the call informing me that I had been selected for the job, I was thrilled, and I felt like I had accomplished something major. I was on the verge of becoming a police officer. I'm not sure if I was happier to get the job or that the intrusive hiring process was over. Shifting into the role of a police officer marked a transition from my career as a paramedic. Although I had developed a certain attachment to my paramedic career, I decided to move forward because it was merely a steppingstone on my path to serving in the police department. This change in direction was somewhat smoother, partly because my wife had grown accustomed to me working in the field of public service. However, my initial enthusiasm for the job vanished quickly as I realized that my expectations of the role did not match the reality I encountered.

Upon being hired, it was time to embark on my journey at the academy. On the very first day, as we sat in our classroom, our class coordinator, a corporal from the Brook Haven Police Department in Georgia, entered the room dressed in what we call "Class A's" – pristine and prestigious uniforms reserved for special occasions. At first glance, he appeared to exude integrity, honor, and a military-like demeanor. However, my later experiences shattered this facade, revealing that he was none of those things, not even close.

During the initial days of the Academy, we were presented with an extensive list of rules, encompassing the do's and don'ts. Among these guidelines, the primary message that was emphasized repeatedly was the importance of always having each other's backs. Initially, I found this concept respectable, a testament to teamwork. Yet, I later realized that this was a constant emphasis on covering up for one another and was merely a method to instill the concept of what I later came to know as the "thin blue line."

The relentless preaching of always having each other's backs was intended to ensure that we would protect each other, even in the face of wrongdoing. Yes, you read that correctly – in the police department not reporting wrongdoing is considered having someone's back. This approach did not align with my principles. I had become a police officer primarily because I thought the career held some degree of prestige and I wanted a job that I thought was better than the one I had. Therefore, I had no intention of jeopardizing it by concealing information for colleagues I barely knew.

Over time, I discovered that being honest within the department held little value; it seemed like certain supervisors did not want certain information disclosed. But the information that wasn't supposed to be disclosed was never hidden from those who were within the department. Looking at this profound revelation closely, this now raised a perplexing question: if the information is not hidden from those within the police department, then who were they hiding it from? The answer became evident – it was you, the public.

I learned the way law enforcement agencies concealed information from the public took several forms. Below is a list of ways things are hidden from the eyes of those of you in the public. Most of these things I'm sure you are already familiar with. Again, these are just some ways information can be hidden or not adequately disclosed to the public:

1. **Limited Transparency**: Police departments may restrict access to certain types of information, such as internal investigations, personnel records, or certain operational procedures. While some of this information is legitimately protected due to privacy concerns or ongoing investigations, excessive secrecy can lead to a lack of public trust.

2. **Slow Release of Information**: Law enforcement agencies might withhold information or release it very slowly, particularly in high-profile cases. This delay can fuel public suspicion and frustration. Timely and accurate information-sharing is crucial to maintain trust.

3. **Selective Information Release**: Sometimes, information may be selectively shared or withheld to shape public perception or protect the image of the department or individual officers. This can include not disclosing misconduct or other negative incidents.

4. **Misleading Statements**: In some cases, law enforcement officials may provide incomplete or misleading information to the public, creating a false narrative or downplaying the significance of an incident.

5. **Legal Protections**: Laws and regulations may protect certain information from public disclosure, such as confidential informants, ongoing investigations, or certain tactics and technologies. While these protections are necessary, they can be abused to hide information unnecessarily.

6. **Lack of Accountability**: If there is a lack of oversight or accountability mechanisms within a police department, there may be no consequences for failing to release information or for intentionally concealing it.

7. **Cultural Norms**: In some cases, there may be a culture within a police department that discourages officers from reporting misconduct or coming forward with information that could harm the reputation of the department or fellow officers.

8. **Use of Force Incidents**: In high-profile cases involving the use of force, video footage, body

camera recordings, or dashcam footage may not be released promptly or may be edited in a way that obscures the full context of an incident.

It's crucial to emphasize that while many law enforcement agencies adopt these practices, not all of them do. There are a few agencies that are committed to transparency and accountability. However, addressing issues related to the release of information to the public is crucial in building and maintaining trust between law enforcement and the communities they serve. Unfortunately, I learned that the community trust factor isn't always the most important thing to an agency.

Back to what I call the academy experience. While many people assume that police academies last six months, the one I attended in Georgia lasted only three months. I can't speak for the entire country, but in Georgia, many academies are of this shorter duration. Consequently, we dove right into the training process from day one due to the limited timeframe. Our daily routines revolved around learning combat techniques and marksmanship skills. I developed exceptional marksmanship skills, although now I can't help but wonder whether this proficiency was a positive or negative aspect, considering that it seemed to be the primary focus which was funded by taxpayer dollars.

Throughout our training, a consistent message was drummed into us: "the world out there is against you," underlining the necessity for constant vigilance. Personally, this message never fully resonated with me because I had family and friends in that same world they were referring to, and none of them harbored harmful intentions towards the police or anyone for that matter. Nevertheless, even though I knew the truth there were moments when I had to remind myself not to fully embrace this mindset and avoid becoming too submerged in it.

We were consistently trained to maintain a heightened state of vigilance, effectively always keeping us on constant alert. This prolonged conditioning amounted to a form of brainwashing over the course of three months. You might wonder how someone can be subjected to brainwashing in such a relatively short time. Well, it's challenging to grasp until you've experienced it firsthand. When immersed in intense training scenarios, engaging in relentless combat simulations, enduring grueling shooting exercises, and repeatedly being told that those you're facing are potentially hostile members of the public, it gradually embeds itself as an undeniable reality. This conditioning is what is used to generate paranoia and it keeps you on edge around the clock. This is the primary reason cops always want to see your hands and order you to not put your hands in your pocket for their safety. Your safety is never their concern.

We were repeatedly instructed never to allow anyone to stand or walk behind us, as they could potentially disarm us or pose a serious threat. Consequently, we were drilled to be on constant guard, always keeping a watchful eye on our surroundings. While I agree with the importance of situational awareness and the seriousness of knowing your surroundings, this type of training only seemed to be designed to foster paranoia. The ultimate goal was to induce enough paranoia to manipulate our actions and cultivate an "us versus them" mentality.

Chapter 3

I Began Questioning the Training

In my online course titled "Surviving the Police," and in my app "Cancel Tyranny," (found at wethepeopleuniversity.com), I talk about the detainment of citizens and the tactics of police during traffic stops. One of these tactics involves the use of questions to make citizens feel obliged to comply. By continuing to question a citizen, it's the hope of the cop that it will confuse them and leave them uncertain about the consequences of non-compliance. This tactic simplifies the process of obtaining identification from each citizen that a cop encounters. This was one of the more disturbing things we learned in the academy. We were being taught methods of how to deceive the public.

For instance, during a traffic stop, if there are passengers in the vehicle besides the driver, after obtaining the driver's ID, we were advised to ask for everyone else's ID while still primarily focusing on the driver. The key was not to demand their identification but to inquire if they had ID on them. This strategy relied on the fact that most passengers would comply and hand over their ID, driven by the belief that they were obligated to comply and a fear of resisting police officers. The point was to obtain their IDs while also protecting ourselves from potential legal consequences. Therefore, if challenged in court the cop can always state, "I only asked if they had ID on them, I never ordered the passenger to give ID".

This is without doubt one of the more cunning tactics we were instructed in during our time at the academy. Yep, we were trained more on how to violate your rights than how to protect them. *I'll be sure to include more insights on dealing with the police at the end of this book*, so please keep reading because I have much more to share. It's important to note that this was a time before the widespread awareness of individual rights and the popularity of auditing videos.

During the training for traffic stops, if you can even call it training, it was emphasized that we should always keep a vigilant eye on everyone in the vehicle because anyone in that vehicle could potentially pose a threat. While I don't fundamentally disagree with this approach – after all, safety is paramount – I firmly believe that public safety should always take precedence over officer safety. As law enforcement officers, we willingly took on the responsibility to protect the God-given and constitutionally protected rights of every citizen.

Once again, it's essential to remember that all these measures were designed to cultivate a paranoid mindset among cadets. For instance, if, during a routine walk down the hallway, an instructor managed to take away your training prop gun from behind, you could expect days of disciplinary physical training (PT). I don't object to the physical training itself, but my concern lay with the paranoid mentality it was intended to cultivate. It struck me as strange that there were never similar disciplinary actions taken when cadets made errors in understanding the law or failed to grasp the information that we were all supposed to learn.

I began to question this approach. Why wasn't the discipline consistent when a cadet made mistakes that could potentially harm a citizen? Nevertheless, I pressed on, hoping to complete the academy, and become a police officer. It wasn't until well after my time at the academy that the true purpose of this training became crystal clear. The training was solely designed to ingrain in us the notion that we needed to be cautious to avoid getting hurt by a member of the public. No one in that academy seemed genuinely concerned with the well-being of citizens.

We were trained to focus on monitoring citizens, with the presumption that they might pose a threat to us. However, we received little, if any, training on the rights of citizens or how to protect and uphold those rights. I'm sad to say when I completed the academy, I was not able to adequately explain why it was important to know the laws between public and private property. Later in my career, it became abundantly clear just how little regard there was for these fundamental principles.

As I transitioned into the Field Training Officer (FTO) phase, I was advised to "fake it until I made it," but I'll talk more about that later. It was apparent that our academy experience had not prioritized a thorough understanding of the law and the rights of citizens. We were essentially spoon-fed test answers to ensure we could pass the state test. Only a handful of us took the initiative to revisit the textbooks and study the material independently to truly grasp the information. Learning the law was not the primary focus. Instead, our attention was directed toward marksmanship, combat training, and the cultivation of a constant sense of paranoia, with the belief that the public posed a threat.

Do you remember the class coordinator, the Corporal from the Brookhaven Police Department in Georgia, whom I mentioned earlier? It was his responsibility to ensure our thorough education during the academy. However, his priorities seemed to lie elsewhere. He showed a conspicuous preference for the female cadets and had a notably poor rapport with me. He exhibited playful behavior toward the women and favored those cadets who ingratiated themselves with him. Since I didn't seek to be part of his circle of minions, I didn't make the cut. This guy repeatedly gave me a hard time until I decided to request a meeting with him.

In that meeting, I threatened to report his conduct to my department's lieutenant and the highest-ranking officer at the academy, the major. Following that discussion, he attempted to be friendly, seemingly aware that we were all privy to his questionable interactions with the female cadets, which he wished to keep under wraps. Frankly, I had no affinity for the man, but I maintained cordiality until the end of the academy. After completing the program, I brought his actions to the attention of my superiors. I'm uncertain about the outcome, but I doubt that it resulted in significant consequences.

Reflecting on those three months at the academy, I can summarize what I gained. I learned that to succeed, one had to be willing to flatter and appease authority figures.

The instructors appeared primarily preoccupied with pursuing relationships with the female cadets. I honed my shooting and combat skills substantially, but unfortunately, I also acquired the ability to deceive citizens to obtain their identification and violate their rights.

The most disheartening revelation was that throughout my time at the academy, I never once heard the phrase "citizens' rights" mentioned. I really don't think I need to elaborate on how terrible that is; after all, isn't that the very reason we pursue this profession? It became unequivocally clear to me that policing was not about serving the public, building community relationships, or safeguarding citizens' rights. It was about asserting control, wielding power, and enforcing compliance.

Chapter 4

Field Training

Now that I've successfully completed my training at the academy, it was now time to take my place within the police department and it was time to delve into the practical aspect of law enforcement. This stage is known as the Field Training phase. During this phase, we put into practice the knowledge and skills we acquired in the academy.

Once I entered this phase I began to train with my new FTO. FTO stands for Field Training Officer, and these experienced officers play a pivotal role in guiding and instructing new recruits on how to effectively carry out their duties. In this phase, we're paired with a designated FTO for a period of 12 weeks. This mentorship was designed for us to gain hands-on experience and learn the intricacies of the job. After completing this initial 12-week training, we switch to another FTO for the same duration. Our performance, speed of learning, and adaptability are supposed to be closely assessed and graded throughout this process. Notice I did say supposed to be.

Allow me to take a step back and recount my experience when meeting the Chief. Prior to commencing my journey at the police academy, I had the privilege of meeting him during the hiring process. Our initial encounter was brief, allowing for only a few words to be exchanged. It wasn't until after I graduated from the academy and officially joined the department as a police officer that I had the chance to get to know him better. During our initial interaction, he left a lasting impression on me. He came across as a principled individual deeply committed to the welfare of his officers. He struck me as the kind of leader who would stand by his team and protect their interests, all while maintaining a commitment to holding his officers accountable for their actions.

During my initial interview with the Chief, he posed a thought-provoking question: "If you encountered my son breaking the law, would you arrest him?" In response, I said, "Sir, if I had probable cause to make the arrest, then I would." His response was positive, and he conveyed that my willingness to uphold the law without bias was a critical factor in his decision to hire me. The Chief shared that his own son had a history of legal troubles with the police but emphasized that family connections should never compromise the performance of our duty. His unwavering commitment to impartiality left a profound impression on me, and I held the utmost respect for his principles and leadership.

Before long, I began to hear about several rumors that were circulating within the police department, not only about several officers in the department but about the Chief also. Remember the individual I mentioned earlier, the class coordinator from the Brookhaven Police Department in Georgia, who played a crucial role in our academy training? Well, it turned out that being able to witness his flirtatious ways with the female cadets was simply a form of training and preparation to help me adapt to the realities I would later encounter as a full-time employee at the department.

I soon learned that issues like infidelity weren't confined to our academy experience; they were widespread across many police departments. Marriages were unraveling among officers, and in hindsight, it's conceivable that personal unhappiness at home might have been a contributing factor to the treatment of citizens. It's highly likely that personal troubles were spilling over into the workplace and had a big impact on the attitude of officers and how they conducted themselves at work. The burden of personal problems could have led to undue stress, which often times found an outlet in their interactions with citizens.

Unfortunately, the rumors about the Chief were that he was using his position for personal gain. People were alleging that he engaged in flirtatious behavior with female officers, using this as a means to promote them. To be honest, I initially found it hard to believe these allegations. Perhaps it was the respect I had developed for him, or maybe it was because I hadn't seen any concrete evidence supporting these claims. I treated these rumors as just that—rumors—until a female police officer confided in me, sharing a similar account.

Let's fast forward a bit. After a couple of years in the department, during which I consistently demonstrated my competence and a strong work ethic, I had the privilege of becoming a Field Training Officer (FTO). I was among the very few officers who never had a complaint filed against them. Some officers had accumulated as many as three complaints within their first six months on the job. Recognizing this, I took great pride in my unblemished record. I had also become a dependable officer in the eyes of my supervisors. In fact, some of them, along with select others, encouraged me to aim for a promotion to the rank of corporal. So, when the opportunity finally arose, I applied for the position of corporal, which is a first-line supervisory role. During the application process, we were required to interview for the position and provide answers to questions related to case law and various scenarios that could arise in the line of duty.

When it was all said and done, I didn't get the corporal position, and I was perfectly fine with that. I told myself that I would try again the next time an opportunity arose. About a week following the interviews and the selection of the chosen candidate, I was called into the training department to meet a new officer I would be responsible for training. Interestingly, this officer had five years of experience as a police officer in Savannah, Georgia, but still required training to understand how our department operated within its specific rules and procedures.

Upon arriving at the training department, I was greeted by the Sergeant and Lieutenant. The Lieutenant appeared visibly disappointed and confided in me that the next corporal position would be given to me. This particular Lieutenant was a member of the interview board responsible for selecting the corporal. During our conversation, I came to understand that I had, in fact, been the stronger candidate for the position. However, contrary to the recommendations made by the interview board, I was not chosen for the role. Hearing this truth was somewhat disheartening.

In a strange turn of events, one of the individuals who sat on the board responsible for selecting the corporal informed me that they had chosen me, but their decision had been overridden by the Chief. In hindsight, I believe it might have been easier for me not to have known the truth and to continue believing that I did not get the position simply because there was a more qualified candidate, rather than hearing what really happened. Discovering the facts of the events that took place left me with a profound sense of unease.

So, why is this significant? Keep reading, and I'll explain. Having realized that I was indeed the most qualified candidate for the corporal position, it was disheartening to know that the individual who was to be my next corporal was not as qualified as I was for the role. What's more disheartening is when the new corporal arrived, guess who was asked to help her, yes her, understand her responsibilities and how to train incoming recruits? That's right, it was me! I found myself taking on the role of ensuring she grasped her duties and how to mentor new officers when they joined the force.

Why did I emphasize "her"? Do you remember the rumors I mentioned earlier, about the Chief's alleged inappropriate behavior towards female officers? It now seemed that these rumors might have some validity to them. Allow me to explain why I think this is a possibility.

As a congratulatory meal, I offered to buy lunch for the new Corporal to congratulate her on her new position. That lunch never happened, unfortunately, we got a call lol. However, we did have a chance to talk later, and she shared some details about the process of accepting the job and her one-on-one meeting with the Chief. She recounted certain actions and comments made by the Chief that she found inappropriate.

Allow me to make this point clear before I move forward. To the best of my knowledge, she had not taken any extra measures to secure the position of Corporal; it was solely the Chief's efforts. I believe he had ulterior motives, hoping that something more might develop from this situation. Therefore, I believe she was entirely innocent in this matter.

As I mentioned earlier, she shared with me that the Chief had made inappropriate comments, and she even caught him casting inappropriate glances at her in a sexual manner when she leaned over to grab a chair from the side of his desk. Hearing her recount these experiences made me reflect on the rumors I had heard about the Chief. Considering the atmosphere of infidelity that was prevalent in the department, I couldn't help but believe that the rumors held some truth. Despite these revelations during our conversation, I chose not to divulge the conversation I had with the Lieutenant in the training department about corporal interviews.

I felt that this situation wasn't her fault, and I didn't want to put her in an awkward position. Consequently, to this day, I've never shared with her what was told and confirmed to me. I maintained my professionalism and respect for her as the corporal, and I carried out my duties in accordance with the expected standards.

So, once again, I came to realize that there were numerous hidden aspects within the department. It wasn't just a place where officers showed up, happy-go-lucky, ready to serve their community. It was a sanctuary for many officers seeking an escape from their home lives, often with backup plans in place at the department, if you catch my drift. The extent of infidelity within this department was deeply troubling. What's even more disheartening is that officers who had previously worked in other departments confirmed that such behavior was a common way of life in many police departments across the country.

As a side note, I should mention why I haven't provided any names or identified the department. The reason is that there's an ongoing legal situation (a lawsuit), and when I informed my legal representation about my intention to publish a book, they advised me to maintain confidentiality until the lawsuit is resolved.

Back to my experiences within the police department. I now realize that the Chief, a man I had deeply respected, was not the person I thought he was. I looked up to him and believed he held his officers accountable. However, I came to realize that he was also among those actively involved in fostering an environment of infidelity within the department. Furthermore, he made a pivotal decision concerning my career that seemed to serve his own personal interests more than anything else. After that revelation, I couldn't view him in the same light.

Nevertheless, he was the Chief, so if I crossed paths with him in the department hallway, I still had to extend courteous greetings and respect his position. After all, he was the Chief.

I suppose these things bothered me deeply because I consider myself a very spiritual individual. I understand that people may hold diverse beliefs and different approaches to life, so I'm not trying to impose my beliefs on anyone. However, spirituality is something I personally value, and when I reflect on the spiritual teachings I adhere to, they emphasize that such behaviors shouldn't occur, especially within the confines of a professional department. Consequently, I made a conscious effort to distance myself from these practices.

Distancing Myself Within the Department

Growing up, I was always advised to surround myself with people I'd wanted to emulate. Within that department, I didn't see anyone I aspired to be like. Many of my colleagues would ask me, "Why don't you ever come hang out with us?" My response was always rooted in my spiritual practices and religious beliefs. There were certain places I did not go to and certain activities I did not take part in. They liked going out to bars and strip clubs. Those were not places I would frequent; a personal preference.

This explanation sufficed for a while, but after some time had passed, I think they began to piece it together. I wasn't being untruthful because what I shared was 100 percent genuine, but at the same time, I had no desire to spend time with those guys. To be honest, the stories I heard from newer officers who did join them for outings were not very positive. It seemed like a ritual where the newer guys footed the bills and served the more seasoned officers, it sounded something like hazing if you ask me. This was a job, not a fraternity—at least, it shouldn't have been, but I learned that's exactly what it was. Shortly after that, I started noticing dirty looks, and it felt like I was the topic of discussion when I wasn't present.

It didn't take long for them to make it clear that they would not help me if I wasn't a part of their inner circle. They wanted to assert their dominance. Let me share a brief incident that occurred during my field training phase to help illustrate the point.

Hung Out to Dry as A Rookie

I commuted to work in my personal vehicle, and before heading to my job, I had to drop my children off at the babysitter. My wife worked in a city called Alpharetta, which was over an hour away from our home. Consequently, our schedules rarely aligned, and we often only had time for a quick kiss in passing. She worked from 7 am to 4 pm, while my shift was from 6 pm to 6 am. Depending on her arrival time, I would either drop the kids off at the babysitter's or quickly pass them to her as I ran out of the door.

One day, as I dropped the kids off at the babysitter's, I was driving back down the road towards work, when a truck backed out into the middle of the road. I paused to see what the driver was doing. It appeared that he had backed out to let another vehicle slowly back out of the long driveway, which wasn't a major issue. However, given that I was running late, I glanced down at the extremely long driveway and noticed that the driver had stepped out of his truck for some reason. In an effort to make it to work on time, I decided to go around him. However, the driver in the road didn't take kindly to my attempt to pass him. He used his truck to cut me off and then stepped out and said, "Can't you see I'm helping another truck back out?"

To provide some context, certain older homes in Georgia have extended driveways, making it challenging for trucks, especially those hauling cargo, to reverse out. Initially, I didn't have a problem with the situation. Again, my perspective changed when I realized that the driver of the truck in the driveway had also exited their vehicle, creating extra time for me to pass.

The issue escalated when I tried to take advantage of the opportunity to maneuver around the truck blocking the road. To be honest, I couldn't understand why he was so agitated. As I mentioned, he got out of his truck and started shouting and berating me.

Therefore, I exited my vehicle and asked him to move his truck. Dressed in full uniform, my presence seemed to surprise him. However, his initial surprise quickly gave way to indifference. He adamantly refused to relocate his truck and attempted to engage in a heated debate with me. He insisted that I wasn't on duty and that I should wait. Furthermore, he asserted that I had no right to pass him.

In response, I calmly explained to him that he had no right to block traffic in such a manner.

Picture this scene: I was new to the department, and suddenly, I found myself in a confrontation with a member of the public. It didn't seem wise to engage in a shouting match with this guy, and I certainly did not want to. Moreover, we were in a somewhat remote location, and I didn't want a verbal dispute to escalate and potentially leave me outnumbered.

I couldn't help but recall my academy training. It started to dawn on me that maybe the training instructors at the academy had a point. Maybe the public did harbor resentment towards us just for wearing the uniform. A barrage of thoughts raced through my mind as this man continued to yell at me. Nevertheless, I remained composed and attempted to engage with him politely. Initially, he was unreceptive to anything I had to say.

In an attempt to resolve the situation, I made a phone call to my department to inform my field training officer and my Sergeant that I was being delayed by a man who refused to move his truck, blocking my path. This area had only one entrance and exit. You might have expected that they would dispatch another unit to at least investigate, but instead, they instructed me to wait.

You can imagine how baffled I was at that moment. First, they attempted to instill as much paranoia as possible into me about dealing with the public, and now, I had an irate citizen standing before me, unlawfully obstructing my way, screaming at me at the top of his lungs, and they were doing absolutely nothing. I was a rookie, stranded in a potentially precarious situation, and their response was simply to wait.

If you, the reader of this book, were to pull your vehicle into the middle of a traffic lane, engage your parking brake, and wait for another vehicle to exit a driveway for an extended period of time, a police officer would promptly issue you a ticket or force you to move at the very least. Blocking traffic in such a manner for an extended period is illegal, and yet, why hadn't they dispatched another unit to investigate why a fellow officer's path was illegally being obstructed?

We've all seen videos where numerous officers arrive for less than nothing. For instance, if someone is recording, it can sometimes lead to the arrival of multiple police officers, sometimes as many as ten, but in this situation, not a single officer arrived to investigate why I, another officer, was unable to leave my position due to the road being illegally blocked? Keep in mind that this situation unfolded over nearly 45 minutes. I could have found myself in trouble, but it became apparent that they simply didn't care.

Remember my earlier mention of not socializing with these guys, the dirty looks, and the sense that I was a topic of discussion when I wasn't present? Well, this incident was a clear message from them to me. "If you don't want to be a part of our group, we won't come to your aid." Thankfully, I continued to apply the de-escalation skills I had acquired while working in the jail system. I persisted in engaging the driver in conversation, and eventually, we were able to communicate. I quickly learned that there was another officer living in the area who habitually sped down the narrow two-lane road, showing little regard for the local residents.

The driver of the truck was upset due to his past experiences with the speeding cop and other officers. He mentioned that he had filed complaints because they were concerned that one day, one of their children might get hurt if this cop continued to speed through their community.

While the situation started one way concerning something else, it ended differently, providing me with an opportunity to listen to a member of the public. The driver was angry, but it wasn't directed at me; it was aimed at the department as a whole. At the time, I didn't know which officer lived in that area, but I made sure to pass the message along to my supervisors when I had the chance.

I'm happy that we were able to have a conversation, and at that point, I saw that this man wasn't a bad guy at all. He appeared to be more of a stand-up individual than some of those who claimed to be my partners but left me in an uncertain situation, not knowing what might happen to me.

Thinking back on it, at that moment, I had no idea how far that situation could have escalated, nor did I know the extent of his dislike or resentment towards the police officers, which made me quite paranoid. I remember seeing the other guy in the truck at the bottom of the driveway, making a phone call, and I had no clue whom he was calling. I didn't know if he was calling others to come, and I wasn't sure if I might be ambushed. But what I did know was this: my supervisors, my field training officer, and the colleagues I worked with in the police department left me hanging.

Once I finally arrived at the department, after my heart-to-heart conversation with the driver, my sergeant asked me what happened. I explained the situation to him and questioned why they did not send anyone to aid me. His response was dismissive, as if nothing significant had occurred. He simply said, "Okay, let's get to work," and that was the end of it. But for me, I never forgot that incident, and I never fully trusted those guys from that point forward. To this day, I wouldn't go out of my way to assist any of them.

Making My Life Miserable

That was just one instance of how those guys tried to send messages. I still had to share the same car with at least one of them, my FTO, and this was on a daily basis. I hated this phase of training, my experience with him was utterly miserable. Every day when I got into the car with my FTO, I didn't speak much. However, one day he encouraged me to open up, saying, "You know, if you're upset, it's okay to talk to me. We're two men spending 12 hours inside the same vehicle. If there's something on your mind, feel free to share, and we can discuss it."

He mentioned this because I was often reserved. The reason for my silence was a lack of trust, particularly after the incident when no one came to my aid or to investigate what was happening to me. So, when he offered to talk, I acknowledged his words and assured him that if anything bothered me, I would let him know. But I told him at that point, I was fine; I just wasn't a talkative person. There was no way I was going to open up to this guy.

Nevertheless, over time, tensions began to rise between us. He had a rather abrasive personality, and while I have thick skin and can handle tough training, this was different. This individual simply did not like me, and he made it evident at every opportunity. I must admit that the feeling was mutual. He would nitpick over the smallest things and attempt to provoke arguments until one day, I showed him that I wouldn't tolerate his disrespect anymore.

One day, while we were driving, I began asking questions to gain a clearer understanding of the boundaries of our jurisdiction. Keep in mind that I was new to the area, having recently moved to Georgia from Florida, and I was still in the process of familiarizing myself with the surroundings. I simply wanted to learn the specifics of our jurisdiction because I believed it was a crucial aspect of performing our duties accurately and effectively. For those unfamiliar with the term jurisdiction, I'll explain it further.

A police jurisdiction refers to the geographical area or territory over which a particular law enforcement agency has authority and responsibility to enforce the law. Police jurisdictions are defined by legal boundaries and are typically established by governmental authorities, such as city, county, state, or federal governments, depending on the level of law enforcement agency.

The specific jurisdiction of a police agency can vary widely. Here are some common examples:

1. **City Police:** Police departments, also referred to as Municipal Police Departments, have jurisdiction within the city limits of a specific municipality/city. They are responsible for enforcing local laws, ordinances, and regulations within that city.

2. **County Sheriff:** County sheriffs and their deputies generally have jurisdiction throughout their respective counties. They often handle law enforcement duties in unincorporated areas (areas not within city limits) and may provide services to municipalities without their own police departments.

3. **State Police/Highway Patrol:** State police or highway patrol agencies typically have jurisdiction across the entire state. They are responsible for enforcing state laws, regulating traffic on state highways, and providing assistance to local law enforcement agencies when necessary.

4. **Federal Agencies:** Federal law enforcement agencies, like the Federal Bureau of Investigation (FBI), the Drug Enforcement Administration (DEA), or the Bureau of Alcohol, Tobacco, Firearms and Explosives (ATF), have jurisdiction over federal crimes that occur nationwide or involve federal interests. They often collaborate with state and local agencies on cases of mutual concern.

5. **Tribal Police:** Tribal police departments have jurisdiction within the boundaries of Native American reservations and tribal lands. They enforce tribal laws and regulations.

6. **Transit Police:** Some metropolitan areas have transit police agencies responsible for enforcing laws and ensuring the safety of passengers on public transportation systems, such as buses and trains.

7. **Specialized Agencies:** There are specialized law enforcement agencies that have jurisdiction in specific areas, such as park rangers in national parks, airport police at airports, and campus police on college campuses.

The boundaries of these jurisdictions are clearly defined by law, and law enforcement officers from one jurisdiction generally do not have the authority to enforce laws in another jurisdiction without specific agreements or circumstances, such as mutual aid agreements or pursuing a suspect who crosses jurisdictional lines during a crime. Cooperation and coordination among different law enforcement agencies are essential for maintaining public safety and enforcing the law effectively. However, as a new officer, understanding the precise boundaries of your jurisdiction can be quite perplexing.

The knowledge of what a jurisdiction is and where ours began and ended did not come from my Field Training Officer (FTO). Instead of helping me understand, he started to display a negative attitude and responded with snarky remarks. After enduring about nine weeks of this guy acting as if he despised me, displaying an unwarranted attitude, and shouting at me without cause on several different occasions, I had reached my breaking point. I'm usually a laid-back person until someone crosses lines, they should never cross, and my FTO had just crossed that line.

I expressed my frustration loudly, aggressively, and with anger, telling him that if he didn't want to be my FTO, he could take me back to the department, and I would exit his car. I also warned him that if he ever screamed at me again, I would make his day very unpleasant (use your imagination). I won't restate everything that I said, but if you think about it, chances are you'll have a fairly accurate picture of how things went. I acknowledge that my response was not the most professional, and I should have handled it differently, but at that moment, I had reached my limit. It had been several weeks, and this individual seemed to derive pleasure from making my life miserable.

Even though my response may not have been ideal, it did lead to a change. After he reported me and we sat down to talk with the Lieutenant (LT), my FTO and I had a heart-to-heart conversation. He explained that he was going through a difficult time at home with his marriage, and he had been bringing his frustrations to work.

Remember when I mentioned that there was a lot of infidelity in the police department? If you connect the dots, you'll see how these issues are intertwined. The personal problems that seep into the workplace not only negatively affect the public when officers become upset;

they also have an impact on fellow officers who are still building their careers.

The conversation between me and my FTO confirmed my belief that many cops are not happy, and they might take out their frustrations on members of the public. He apologized, and for the remainder of the FTO phase, we attempted to be at least cordial.

I went through the academy's rigorous training, which involved a lot of shouting, and I found that the FTO phase was no different. In my opinion, both phases seemed to be designed to manipulate individuals. This perspective comes from my experience serving in the military and understanding the nature of basic training. While the military's basic training is designed to build and strengthen individuals, I felt that police basic training was geared more towards mental manipulation.

As a graduated police officer working in a police department, being trained by an FTO who brought his home life frustrations to work and enjoyed tormenting others, there was no justification for screaming at adults and trying to belittle them simply because he felt he could. While I accepted being yelled at when I made a mistake, I believed there was a significant difference between that and being screamed at just for the sake of it.

At first, I believed my struggles during the FTO phase were unique to me because of my reluctance to associate with most of the other officers. I believed that they had discovered I wasn't interested in joining their inner circle, which could be why they didn't have a favorable opinion of me. However, I started conversing with other rookies going through the FTO phase, and they shared that they were facing similar challenges with their FTOs.

They also hated how they were being treated. The environment was not conducive to learning; it felt more like paying your dues to be part of a particular fraternity as I mentioned earlier. The only problem was that I started to go against the grain. I didn't believe people should be treated so poorly, even if they were rookies. I held the same belief about law enforcement; it didn't matter that we were rookies; we were still human beings. This phase felt more like hazing, and due to how they were treated, some of those rookies went on to display similar behaviors towards members of the public.

This job was the first one that made me feel absolutely miserable. I dreaded going to work, not because of the job itself or the community I served, but because of the person I had to spend 12 hours a day with. Being stuck for this long inside of a small car with someone you do not like is a miserable feeling. It was a constant back-and-forth, and even though we managed to maintain a semi cordial relationship after my outburst, the damage was done, and I still despised spending 12 hours a day with him.

What made the entire experience worse was the extensive infidelity within the department, the mistreatment we received, the inadequate training, and the expectation that you had to socialize with these guys outside of work, or they would make your job a living hell.

Living In the World of Tyranny

The Ridiculous Actions of Cops

I remember one day when my assigned FTO was sick, and I was placed with another FTO who had a reputation for writing tons tickets daily, earning him the nickname "Traffic Nazi." One day, he suddenly slammed on the brakes, turned on the lights and sirens, and jumped out of the car. I sat there, baffled, and wondering what was happening since he hadn't said a word. He told me to get out of the car urgently, and I complied, expecting a major incident. However, when I asked him what was going on, he informed me that the lady in the truck next to us at a red light wasn't wearing her seatbelt.

I couldn't believe it. I was waiting for Ashton Kutcher to jump out and tell me I was being pranked. It was absolutely unnecessary and infuriating. We had jumped out into the middle of traffic to confront an elderly woman who was driving a pickup truck and helping another family member move their furniture. He demanded she roll down her window and proceeded to investigate why she wasn't wearing her seatbelt. While I understand the importance of seatbelt enforcement, this incident was a gross overreaction and put everyone involved at risk.

My FTO phase was pretty terrible, and the supervisors seemed to hold FTOs in high regard, believing they could do no wrong. Through this experience, I gained awareness of the tactics used – instill paranoia, control minds through intimidation, and ultimately manipulate the actions of every cop, much like what we experienced during our academy training.

Understanding the Manipulation

The flaw in this training approach was that I was always one to ask questions and not blindly follow orders. So, controlling my actions didn't work out as intended. I would estimate that about 60% of the officers in the department would unquestioningly follow orders. It was known that any questions or doubts about directives would be met with resistance.

During one of my FTO days I recall my FTO expressing surprise, saying, "Wow, that's really good. I've never had a trainee or rookie who reads as much as you do." He was referring to my habit of reading the Georgia law codes, which are referred to as O.C.G.A. or Official Code of Georgia Annotated. What he didn't realize at the time was that I was reading to avoid talking to him. This FTO had treated me poorly every chance he got, and it turns out he treated all rookies the same way. He had a reputation for treating his trainees poorly and making them feel worthless. Later, I discovered something shocking: he had a trophy wall in his home. On this wall, he displayed the name badges of every rookie he had driven to quit the force. I overheard him sharing this information with a dispatcher during one of our visits to dispatch, and I was disgusted. It became clear that he was trying to make me quit.

As time went on, I noticed that I was excluded from certain group events. It didn't bother me because I didn't want to be around those guys anyway, but I couldn't help but notice the secretive and exclusive nature of these gatherings. Looking back, I realized that they used various manipulative tactics, including exclusion, to manipulate and control our actions. They wanted us to feel the need to be part of their fraternity, the "thin blue line gang" as I later came to know it. For those who were easily influenced and unable to think for themselves, they would do anything to gain acceptance.

This was their way of legally forcing officers to comply with their wishes. Make you feel isolated until you agree to be in their circle and watch their back. They started in the academy by creating a false sense of paranoia about the public's hostility toward us. Then they made us feel like we were nothing without them, cultivating a deep desire to fit in because being separate was made intentionally uncomfortable. If they could make us feel this way, they could make us do almost anything as long as we desired to be part of their exclusive club.

Chapter 5

My Interactions as A Cop

Having completed my Field Training, the final step before becoming an independent police officer was a discussion with the captain. This was something that I really did not want to do. I had to have this conversation due to a disagreement with my Field Training Officer (FTO) who then reported me to the Lieutenant. Rewinding back just a little, the conversation with my Lieutenant wasn't so bad. We had to have a conversation about my grievances with my FTO. Surprisingly, the Lieutenant asked my FTO to leave the room, opting for a one-on-one conversation with me. During the talk, he acknowledged that my FTO's actions and words were indeed unnecessary, and they were not an isolated incident.

However, despite his understanding, he felt compelled to report the matter to the captain. Now, as the day arrived for me to work independently, I found myself in the captain's office recounting the episode with my FTO from several weeks ago. It was apparent that the captain was not inclined to support my perspective. Throughout the conversation, it felt as though he was merely waiting for me to make a mistake, providing a pretext for disciplinary action. He brought up something I had mentioned to the Lieutenant during our previous discussion, and that was my dissatisfaction with the poor treatment that I had been receiving since being at the department.

I explained that I had chosen this department over other job offers, not to boast, but to convey my desire to work at this department because I felt it was a good fit. Unfortunately, the captain misconstrued my words, accusing me of arrogance and suggesting that I believed I had better options elsewhere. Realizing I was in a no-win situation, I chose to remain silent. This further reinforced my perception that FTOs were infallible, and rookies like me were always in the wrong.

With that, I left the captain's office, eager to begin my career as a police officer but more eager to simply get away from everyone. Despite the captain's attitude, I didn't let it bother me. I was just determined to simply get away and have some breathing room. Now I was on a new journey, and I was about to learn some valuable lessons, However I wasn't too concerned, again I just wanted to get away.

My next phase was called the Shadowing Phase. This is where my FTO would meet me on calls just in case I needed assistance. I would drive my vehicle and he would drive his. They would gauge things like how long it took me to arrive at the scene and how long it took me to complete the call. Typically, this phase lasted 12 weeks, but my FTO shortened my shadow phase by 11 weeks, because he stated that he was confident in my abilities.

Surprisingly, when I ended my shadow phase after just one week, there were no sarcastic comments or condescending attitudes. Initially, I assumed he was as weary of me as I was of him. However, to my astonishment, he expressed his belief that I would excel as a police officer and didn't think he needed to oversee me any longer. He pointed out my adaptability and was notably impressed by my commitment to understanding state laws to enhance my role as a law enforcement officer, even though my primary intent was to avoid speaking to him. I was taken aback but genuinely appreciated his recognition.

Now I am out and on my own and I finally feel free. One day, as a solo officer with no FTO or shadow, I received a call regarding a woman living in a trailer who believed someone was hiding beneath it. Once I arrived, she advised me when the shooting started the man ran and hid under her trailer. I radioed dispatch to report the situation and proceeded to gather more information from the frightened woman. Her anxiety was intense as she recounted her story.

I attempted to locate the man by calling out to him and shining my flashlight under the trailer. However, he remained silent and hard to spot. When I asked the woman how long he had been there, she claimed he had been hiding under there since the start of World War II. Yes, you read that correctly, World War II! At that moment, it became clear that this woman was not mentally stable. She went on to share stories of surviving nuclear bombs dropped on her trailer, and it was apparent that her delusions were escalating.

Realizing the extent of her mental illness, I assured her that the man had left for a nearby shelter. I also attempted to ease her fears concerning more nuclear attacks. I told her that the war had come to an end, and she had nothing else to worry about. I left the scene, feeling a mix of empathy and sadness for her.

This marked my first encounter with someone suffering from mental illness, and while I provided temporary comfort, it raised questions about the lack of resources for individuals in her situation. I later learned that her family occasionally checked on her well-being, but it left me pondering the need for more substantial support for those grappling with mental health issues.

She Touched My Heart

During a night well into my policing career, I conducted a routine traffic stop and quickly realized that the driver had neither an updated registration nor insurance for her vehicle. In Georgia, driving without insurance typically meant the vehicle should be towed. As I approached her window, I noticed her trembling with fear. I requested her driver's license, which she handed over willingly. I then informed her that I could confirm that she did not have insurance, to which she then openly admitted.

Curious about her situation, I inquired why was she driving, fully aware of the consequences of driving without insurance in Georgia. She replied that she had to go to work and had just picked up her 12-year-old daughter after finishing her shift. She had also stopped at Walmart to buy some food because they were both hungry and they had nothing to eat at home. Glancing inside her car, I noticed a couple of small bags of groceries, a hardhat, and a construction vest—items suggesting she was likely employed in a warehouse or construction job. In the passenger seat, her daughter was visibly upset, likely anticipating the imminent loss of their vehicle.

I believed her story and genuinely wanted to help her. I refrained from speaking to her daughter since she was probably already aware that their car was at risk of being towed. It was at that moment I found myself questioning my role as a police officer. I was willing to face danger but making life more difficult for people who were struggling to get out of an already hard situation seemed fundamentally wrong. I advised the driver to try obtaining insurance on the spot, hoping to avoid towing her vehicle. She agreed to make an attempt.

Returning to my patrol vehicle, I radioed dispatch that I was code 4, indicating that everything was okay at the scene. Dispatch periodically checked on officers during calls, and I wanted them to know that I was fine despite the stop taking longer than usual due to my desire to assist rather than tow her vehicle.

After about 15 minutes, I returned to her window, and she informed me that she couldn't find anyone to lend her the money for insurance. As much as I wanted to help, I was in a financial struggle myself and couldn't provide the funds. Of course, I didn't share this with her, but I mentioned it now because I understood her predicament. Ultimately, after nearly 45 minutes at this traffic stop, I made the bold decision to allow her to leave.

This decision was bold because, according to protocol, vehicles without insurance should be towed when seen on a public road in Georgia. I was nervous about my decision because if she left and got into a car accident, my prior interaction with her would be on record, leading to questions about why I hadn't towed the vehicle. Therefore, I issued her a stern warning.

I had to make sure the warning was stern because I truly had no alternative solution in this situation. It was either make sure she got the point so I could let her go or tow her vehicle and I had already made up my mind that I was not going to do that. I instructed her to drive straight home and added that I would patrol the area to ensure she complied. If I saw her on the road again, I assured her that I would indeed tow her vehicle. She followed my advice, and I was relieved not to tow her vehicle. My intention was to make her aware of the seriousness of the situation without causing unnecessary hardship or risk to my own job.

With all of this in mind, as I strive to have a compassionate approach toward the public and assist people, it's disheartening to note that the higher-ups in my department had entirely different intentions. Their plans involved increasing traffic stops and conducting more searches, ultimately leading to more rights violations, all under the guise of pursuing some goal which was motivated by food. Brace yourselves, as the following details may seem rather absurd.

The Steak Dinner Scandal: Unraveling the Myth and Secret Scheme"

Many citizens have asked me if there is a citation or arrest quota that exists within the police departments. It became clear that a long-standing false belief had become deeply ingrained in not only the citizens of our city, but in the minds of many citizens nationwide. I must admit that this is merely myth, widely embraced among the public, that had led many to subscribe to a belief that law enforcement officers operated under a hidden quota, a persistent notion that they were under pressure to meet a specific target number of tickets and or arrest. This misconception had woven itself into the fabric of the community and the minds of many shaping perceptions and influencing how citizens viewed the actions of the police force.

However, being a police officer working from within the department, I was privy to the facts. Despite being commonly accepted by the public, this idea had no foundation, and not only that, but it was also illegal. It is imperative to understand that the Chief of Police does not have the legal authority to require officers to meet any ticketing or arrest quota. Yet, despite the undeniable facts, a peculiar and secretive scheme took place within the department in which I now worked. A secretive scheme motivated by an unusual incentive: food. This covert operation was driven by a desire for something as simple as a meal, creating an absurd scenario within our law enforcement community.

The idea that officers thought they could get around legal stipulations by offering food as a reward versus ordering cops to write citations or make arrest was not only silly, but many individuals were ok with it. Cops were being bribed with cookouts, yes, cookouts, to entice them into violating the rights of citizens. Yes, it may sound astonishing, but officers were being enticed with sizzling steaks and mouthwatering barbecue delights in exchange for more traffic stops and vehicle searches.

It was believed that this peculiar plan was orchestrated by one of our Lieutenants, a high-ranking officer within the department. Shortly after this took place the Lieutenant was caught on the department surveillance video offering rewards to fellow officers in exchange for ramping up their efforts in various law enforcement activities. The Lieutenant's rationale behind this plan was rooted in the belief that such actions would create the illusion that the department was intensifying its crackdown on crime, thereby boosting its public image.

However, beneath the surface, the reality was quite different. The consequences of this scheme were manifold and deeply concerning. First and foremost, it meant that officers were susceptible to bribery, compromising their integrity and the trust placed in them by the community. Moreover, this plan resulted in the department's focus shifting away from the actual criminal activities, which lead to a crackdown on law-abiding citizens who were caught in the crossfire. Innocent citizens found themselves facing unwarranted traffic stops and unnecessary searches, while their rights were consequently trampled upon in the process. So, what seemed to be a sincere attempt to combat crime turned out to be a tangled web of deceit spun by police officers, individuals who had taken an oath to uphold the constitution and safeguard the rights of every citizen.

Fortunately, this secretive scheme didn't remain concealed for long. The story was leaked to a news reporter who decided to expose the truth, holding the department accountable for its actions. It was through this news report that I, too, became aware of the shocking situation.

I wasn't on duty during the bribery scandal; it had unfolded during a shift when I wasn't at work. However, I soon learned that it was one of the rookies, who had been subjected to mistreatment within the department, who had courageously brought the story to light. I suspect that this might have been a form of retaliation by this specific rookie. To be honest, I really didn't care who revealed the truth; I was just grateful that someone had the courage to do so.

As this scandal was slowly brought to light, it sent shockwaves throughout our department to those officers who were unaware of it, it became a source of profound embarrassment. Not only that, but the citizens seized the opportunity to criticize us, ridiculing our willingness to compromise our principles for a mere steak dinner. Also, the sheriff's office did not miss their opportunity to poke fun at our department every chance they got. The humiliation was palpable, even for someone like me who had unwittingly been a part of this absurdity.

As the news of the steak dinner scandal spread, the Chief of Police was interviewed by the news stations giving him an opportunity to explain himself. In an attempt to distance himself from the controversy, he boldly denied any prior knowledge of the situation until it was told to him by his command staff. However, within the department, it was not a secret that he had not only been aware of it but had also played a role in conceiving the idea, casting a dark shadow over his leadership.

Despite the glaring misconduct, when the Lieutenant was caught, the Chief's response was to transfer him to another position within the department, apparently presenting it as a form of punishment. However, to those of us who scrutinized the situation closely, it became clear that this move was nothing more than a smokescreen, a calculated effort to create the illusion of accountability where, in reality, there was none. To compound the situation, this supposed punishment turned out to be merely a short-lived measure, just long enough to let the memory of the situation fade. Afterward, the Lieutenant resumed his duties as if nothing had ever occurred.

The decision to transfer the Lieutenant raised significant doubts about the department's commitment to addressing serious misconduct. Instead of taking decisive action to hold individuals accountable for their actions and to restore public trust, the Chief, as the head of the department, simply made an attempt to sweep the issue under the rug. It wasn't just me; but certain members of the department and the community shared the same perspective. I soon noticed that this was the norm and a culture that had been cultivated long before my arrival in the department. It gave the impression that the higher-ups were more interested in avoiding public scrutiny than in addressing the underlying problems within the department.

This insignificant form of discipline did little to ease the concerns of officers and citizens alike. It left a lingering sense of injustice and eroded confidence in the department's ability to self-regulate and maintain integrity. I suppose it's what we've all come to recognize as the classic "I'll investigate myself, and unsurprisingly, find no wrongdoing" scenario. The incident served as a stark reminder that true accountability and transparency does not truly exist in most departments. Contrary to prevailing belief, I hold onto the hope that there are still some departments out there that maintain their integrity in their operations.

My Disappointment in the Chief

As time passed, I began to notice a transformation in the man I had once deeply respected—The Chief, and the previously-mentioned situation at hand only exacerbated my evolving perception of him. His true character was gradually becoming more evident to me, and it was a revelation that stirred mixed emotions within me.

When I first entered the department, I regarded The Chief as the standard of integrity and leadership. His words carried weight, and his actions appeared to be rooted in a profound commitment to justice and upholding the law. As I previously stated, my deep respect for The Chief initially took root when he made it abundantly clear that if I were ever to witness his own son committing a crime, I should carry out an arrest without any consideration for their family ties. I admired his dedication to our community and believed he upheld the highest standards within our ranks.

However, as days turned into weeks and weeks into months, I began to notice facets of his personality that had previously eluded my attention. It was as though a curtain was slowly being drawn back, revealing a different aspect of his character. This evolving perspective exposed inconsistencies in his behavior and decision-making that prompted me to question my initial impressions.

There were situations where it seemed that his primary concern was safeguarding the department's reputation rather than addressing serious internal issues. Situations such as the one I described earlier and those I'll discuss later in this book. It became increasingly evident that he was willing to downplay or even disregard instances of misconduct when it served his own interests or preserved the department's image.

The gradual revelation of these facets of his character left me feeling disillusioned and disheartened. The Chief, once a symbol of honor and integrity in my eyes, was now displaying a willingness to compromise on those very principles when it suited his needs. It was a stark reminder that individuals can undergo a transformation, and that the image we hold of someone may not always align with their true nature.

As I struggled with this evolving perspective, it served as a valuable lesson about the complexities of human nature and the significance of maintaining a discerning eye, even when it comes to individuals we hold in high regard. This emphasizes that genuine leadership and integrity are not merely a matter of words and appearances but are defined by consistent actions and an unwavering commitment to the values that we cherish.

I loved Interacting with the People

Despite my evolving thoughts about the Chief, I was still here to do a job. I found delight in interacting with the community. It was a part of the job I loved, despite my introverted nature. I loved engaging with the community and helping individuals in need. One memorable incident involved responding to a call from an elderly woman who was having trouble with her grandson. Upon arriving, I initially took on the role of the stern officer to get his attention. However, after gaining his trust, he confided in me about some distressing family matters that no child should have to endure.

To support him, I gave him my word. I told him I would meet him at the basketball court on my days off to play ball with him. He was skeptical at first, but when I showed up, he was a believer. We began to play basketball and I played with unwavering competitiveness, even though he managed to beat me every game. He would later recognize me in the community and shout my name from afar, expressing his gratitude and connection with me.

Aren't these the reasons we become police officers, to serve and protect the community, build relationships, and combat crime? It's what I signed up for and what I thought my career in law enforcement would entail. However, as I'll explain further in this book, the reality of the job began to diverge from these ideals, leading to both love and frustration with my career.

Chapter 6

Traffic Stops

Keep in mind that I just told you about the lowdown scandal that the higher-ups at the police department planned in order to violate the rights of citizens. Given the unsettling events I've shared, it becomes absolutely vital that you possess a thorough understanding of your rights. The reason is that there are individuals within police departments who are not only aware of the nuances of the law but are also prepared to exploit any gaps in your knowledge for their gain.

In many cases, when facing unexpected encounters with the police, these individuals might attempt to use your lack of knowledge to their benefit. They may employ tactics that could catch you off guard or encourage you to accidentally surrender your rights. This is why having a firm grasp of your rights becomes a powerful tool in protecting yourself and safeguarding your liberties in any interaction with police.

By being well-informed about your rights, you empower yourself to confidently navigate such situations, ensuring that your rights are upheld, and that you're not unwittingly drawn into a compromising position. In essence, knowledge becomes your protection against potential deception, ensuring that you can assert your rights when needed and protect yourself from unwarranted infringements.

Working as a cop, it became apparent that every person should have a grasp of traffic law basics. Such knowledge not only serves to protect your rights but also safeguards the rights of others. As I developed my online course, "Surviving the Police," (Found at WeThePeopleUniversity.Com) I recognized the necessity of educating individuals about the intricacies of traffic stops.

One of the critical lessons I teach in the course, specifically under the section titled "Traffic Stop Basics," pertains to when cops can and cannot search your vehicle. I shed light on the clever tricks they utilize to chip away at your rights during these encounters.

Police officers often use trick questions during traffic stops, making it essential to recognize that engaging in conversation with them can be a double-edged sword. Allow me to walk you through some of these trick questions cops ask:

1. **"DO YOU KNOW WHY I PULLED YOU OVER?"** On the surface, this question might seem like a simple question, and the officer is only seeking clarification on the infraction committed. However, it's a common tactic to catch drivers off guard and extract information before they can assert their rights under the Fifth Amendment. Remember you have the right to remain silent. Any response to this question may be used against you in court. For instance, if you respond with, "Because I ran a red light," that now becomes a record of admission that can and will seriously harm your defense in court. You are under no obligation to answer any

questions by police accept when state laws may deem it necessary. Example: in a "Duty to Inform State" if an officer asked if there are any firearms in the vehicle you must answer that question.

2. **"WHERE ARE YOU COMING FROM?"** This question might appear innocent as the cop pretends like he is simply attempting to have friendly conversation, but it's a vital part of the officer's investigative process. It helps him to gather information about your location and activities before the stop. If an officer suspects you're under the influence, your responses, such as "coming from lunch," "a bar," or "a club," can raise suspicions and negatively impact the outcome of the traffic stop. Remember to remain silent and only give the pertinent documentation that is required such as driver's license, registration, and insurance.

3. **"CAN I SEARCH YOUR VEHICLE?"** There's a common misconception that police officers have the blanket authority to search vehicles during a traffic stop. However, this is not true. The officer must have probable cause, consent, or a warrant before he is able to conduct a vehicle search during a traffic stop.

Therefore, it's crucial not to be misled into thinking that you are obligated to grant permission for a vehicle search just because a police officer request it. Cops often will pose the question in a way that implies compliance is mandatory, but it's critical to stand firm on your rights and never permit any violations of those rights. Now, let's delve deeper into the topic of searches during traffic stops:

When an officer asks to search your vehicle, and you choose to decline, it's crucial to immediately follow up by asserting your Fifth Amendment right to remain silent. Many officers may try to engage you in conversation, often saying things like, "If you have nothing to hide, then you won't have anything to worry about." They don't use this line without reason; they're well aware that countless citizens have fallen for this age-old tactic repeatedly.

This statement can pose a dual challenge for two primary reasons. First, it may trap you in a conversation that could be deemed consensual in court. This could potentially diminish your legal protection because it delays the commencement of the reasonable time clock, as established in the case Rodriguez vs. the United States which states an officer is only permitted to detain an individual for the duration necessary to issue a citation or a warning. Any extension of the stop beyond a reasonable timeframe for addressing the traffic violation must be supported by probable cause. If a traffic stop is prolonged without the presence of probable cause, it constitutes a violation of an individual's Fourth Amendment rights.

If you allow yourself to engage in conversation with the officer from a legal standpoint, he could argue that he did not unreasonably detain you during a traffic stop for an extended duration. He could and most likely will assert that the conversation was consensual, even though a reasonable person might not have felt he was free to leave.

The background of the case Rodriguez v the United States is found below.

On March 27, 2012, in Nebraska, a K-9 police officer initiated a traffic stop on a vehicle driven by Dennys Rodriguez. The reason for the stop was Rodriguez's vehicle was veering onto the highway's shoulder. After conducting a traffic stop and issuing a written warning, the officer requested permission to conduct a K-9 dog sniff around Rodriguez's vehicle. Rodriguez declined this request, but the officer instructed him to exit the vehicle and proceeded to walk the police dog around it. During the inspection, the dog alerted to the presence of drugs, ultimately leading to the discovery of a substantial quantity of methamphetamine.

Rodriguez subsequently took legal action to suppress the evidence obtained during the search, contending that the K-9 search violated his Fourth Amendment right, which protects individuals from unreasonable seizures. However, the district court rejected his motion. Upon further appeal, the United States Court of Appeals for the Eighth Circuit upheld the lower court's decision, asserting that the search was constitutional. Their rationale was that the brief delay incurred before employing the police dog did not unreasonably prolong the stop which they deemed lawful.

The pivotal question at hand revolved around whether utilizing a K-9 unit following the completion of a traffic stop, absent reasonable suspicion of criminal activity, constituted a violation of the Fourth Amendment's prohibition against unreasonable searches and seizures.

As per the United States Supreme Court's ruling, the answer to the question was affirmative. Justice Ruth Bader Ginsburg delivered the majority opinion, supported by a 6-3 vote. The Court determined that deploying a K-9 unit after concluding an otherwise lawful traffic stop exceeded the reasonable time required to handle the initial matter, thereby violating the Fourth Amendment's prohibition against unreasonable searches and seizures.

The Court emphasized that the allowable duration of a stop hinges on the mission it seeks to accomplish. Once the mission is fulfilled, the authority for the stop concludes. Any seizure unrelated to the stop's purpose remains lawful only if it does not significantly extend the stop's duration. While the use of a K-9 unit may extend the stop only slightly, it cannot be considered directly related to the mission of a routine traffic stop and is thus deemed unlawful.

In light of this, when you're pulled over by the police, it's important to provide only the necessary information required for them to conduct the traffic stop's essential business. Beyond that point, you are under no legal obligation to respond to any further questions or statements. By doing so, you allow them the opportunity to potentially overstep their bounds and violate your rights, particularly by unlawfully detaining you during a traffic stop once they've had a reasonable amount of time to issue a citation or warning.

The duration considered reasonable will depend on the specifics of the traffic stop. For instance, if you're pulled over for a window tint violation, there is no justification for such a stop to last as long as 45 minutes. A reasonable duration for this type of stop might be closer to 15 minutes. However, if you're pulled over because you and your vehicle match the description of a recent bank robbery in the area, then the stop may understandably extend well beyond the time required for a window tint violation. The court has not provided an exact timeframe but rather emphasized that the duration should be deemed reasonable, leaving the interpretation of what constitutes a reasonable timeframe to be subjective.

How the Traffic Stop Is Conducted

In the world of law enforcement, a traffic stop is far more than a routine procedure; it's an ongoing investigation. Every time an officer pulls you over, it's vital to remember that they have not initiated the traffic stop for a friendly game of golf. While many individuals grasp this reality, there are still those who fall prey to the good cop façade.

Let's delve into what typically happens during a traffic stop from the perspective of an officer.

The process begins with running the vehicle registration information to identify the driver. The next step is selecting a suitable location to pull the vehicle over. This part of the stop holds great significance for all officers since he or she can find themselves positioned outside of their patrol vehicle, exposed to passing cars traveling at speeds high enough to pose a serious risk of injury or even fatality.

As the vehicle comes to a stop, the patrol car is positioned strategically behind it at an angle, always prepared for any potential security threats. For instance, during our brain washing, I meant during our training at the police academy, we were instructed that citizens could potentially pose an immediate threat, capable of drawing a weapon and opening fire within a fraction of a second. While there's some truth in this notion, it was employed to instill more paranoia into the officers.

In cases where darkness obscures visibility, officers use their vehicle's lights to momentarily blind the driver, allowing them to observe without being easily seen. After these initial steps, the officer promptly exits the patrol car and begins scanning the vehicle thoroughly. Every occupant in the back and passenger seats are noted and labeled potential threats, and if there are several individuals, an officer will immediately call for backup.

A subtle but significant tactic is discreetly touching the vehicle's brake light. This leaves fingerprints for future identification in case something tragic happens to the officer. Finally, the officer positions him or herself at either the driver's side or passenger's side window, depending on their suspicions.

When a cop is positioned outside the vehicle during a traffic stop, his primary focus is to examine the interior of the vehicle for any potential signs of illegal activity. This procedure is called the Plain View Doctrine, a legal concept that gained official recognition from the U.S. Supreme Court in 1968 through the case of Harris vs. the United States, following its initial articulation in Coolidge v. New

Hampshire. Additionally, if you observe a police officer leaning closer to your vehicle window, it's likely they are conducting what's known as a sniff test, checking for the presence of illegal drugs or alcohol inside the vehicle.

All these actions are part of the investigative process during a traffic stop. While it may appear that a police officer is engaged in casual conversation, it's crucial to understand that law enforcement officers are trained to approach these encounters with high suspicion. Cops are taught to operate under the assumption that citizens may have hidden motives or illegal items that they may be attempting to conceal. Cops approach every citizen with this type of mindset due to the training we received and to assure all grounds of the investigation are covered.

For those looking to gain a deeper understanding of their rights and how to deal with police, I strongly recommend enrolling in my online course, Surviving the Police (Found at WeThePeopleUniversity.Com). My course covers essential information about your rights and provides valuable insights on how to interact with cops effectively, ensuring your rights are protected during these encounters.

Chapter 7

A Quick Glance at Hypocrisy

I've often been asked, "Abiyah, have you ever worked alongside 'bad cops' when you were a police officer? You know the ones that break all of the laws but never seem to face any consequences." The answer is yes. Even though I'm no longer a cop, during my time on the force, I did encounter colleagues whose actions raised concerns. People often inquire if I reported these bad apples, and once again, the answer is yes. I felt compelled to do so because all the reasons I joined the police force were far from what I had witnessed within the department.

Cops Attempting to Beat the Snot Out of Each Other

Behind the closed doors of the department, often there is an incident that the public does not get a chance to see or hear about. Allow me to explain this with a specific example. We had an officer in our department who served as a K-9 officer, and one day, he nearly engaged in a huge fight with his shift's lieutenant. It took the intervention of five or six officers to separate them. One might wonder how cops who are expected to uphold the law and maintain order could have such a hard time keeping themselves in order.

It became even more perplexing when, a few minutes later, they left the patrol room, where the pre-shift meetings are held, got into their cars, and went out to police the neighborhood. Yes, it was rather interesting that the two cops who moments ago seemed intent on literally killing each other were now entrusted with the responsibility of enforcing the law, including the laws of assault and battery. That seemed rather funny but not so funny if you ask me. My first thought was if they encountered one of the members of the public acting in the same manner as they were, the situation would most likely not end in the same way. That unfortunate citizen would have been arrested without question.

Failing to Follow Policy Claimed a Life

Now, let me recount a story that continues to weigh heavily on my heart whenever I discuss it, and there are several compelling reasons for this. The first reason is I firmly believe that this situation could have been entirely prevented. Secondly, it resulted in the tragic loss of a young life. And thirdly, the way in which this situation was handled by our department showed a profound lack of concern from both the department and the officer involved. The incident I'm referring to involves the untimely death of a young girl, for which a police officer in my former department shares significant responsibility.

Again, this incident reflects not only a tragic loss but also the department's poor response to it. Recalling this story is truly disturbing for me, especially when considering how it was perceived within the department and the fact that it was regarded as a minor issue. However, I will explain, an officer who was recklessly speeding down the road, violating police department policy in the process was involved in creating a car accident that claimed the life of a young girl.

Some of you may know there are certain criteria for initiating a high-speed chase or, as we called it in our department, a 1080. Pursuing a suspect had to be justified by policy, and it couldn't be for a minor offense. Typically, the crime had to be a felony to ensure the safety of the public, as we understood that pursuing a vehicle could pose risks to innocent bystanders. However, in this incident, the officer falsely informed the supervisor via the radio, that he wasn't chasing the vehicle; he was merely trying to catch up to it.

The distinction between an officer merely trying to catch up to a vehicle and actively chasing it is crucial. You might be curious about where this particular officer picked up the deceptive tactic of radio communication, using the "I'm trying to catch up to one" narrative instead of explicitly stating he was actively involved in a 1080. If you haven't guessed it already, this tactic was actually taught during our time at the police academy. Not so surprisingly, our esteemed instructor himself admitted to employing this trick multiple times, allowing him to engage in high-speed chases when it wasn't warranted, thus recklessly putting the public at risk. His rationale was that by stating he was trying to catch up to a vehicle, it created a record suggesting he wasn't technically in pursuit, providing a potential defense in case the matter ended up in court.

During this incident, the officer didn't activate his lights or sirens, which is another violation of policy, as he sped through the streets. I would assume drivers on the road may not have noticed him until it was too late, potentially narrowly avoiding several accidents. In this tense situation, the driver of the pursued vehicle reacted by accelerating in an attempt to evade the officer. Tragically, a car accident occurred, and a 16-year-old girl sitting in the passenger seat lost her life upon impact.

There has been much discussion about this incident, and I've heard arguments from both sides. Some say it's the cop's fault, while others place the blame on the driver, arguing that he shouldn't have tried to flee from the officer. However, what remains clear is that had the officer adhered to department policy, this young girl would still be alive today.

It was said that the 1080 was initiated due to a suspended license, which served as the initial justification for pursuing the vehicle. However, it's important to note that a suspended license, is categorized as a misdemeanor in the state of Georgia and does not merit an officer jeopardizing the safety of the general public by engaging in a high-speed chase. This prompts the question: Why was this particular officer so enthusiastic about pursuing a vehicle that hadn't committed a serious offense, like a felony? The problem lies in the eagerness of some officers to make arrests and issue tickets, almost as if they're treating it like a game, hunting for prey. During our pre-shift meetings in the patrol room, it was not uncommon to hear someone shout, "Let's go make some arrests!"

Now, let me explain my own perspective and approach. Despite being part of that group, making arrests for the sake of making them was never exciting for me. If I arrested someone, they genuinely deserved it, as I wasn't driven by the thrill of increasing my arrest numbers. On quiet nights with empty roads and nothing pressing to attend to, I won't deny that I occasionally watched YouTube videos, which is how I stumbled upon the auditing community.

The concept of hunting down innocent people for the sake of boosting arrest statistics didn't sit well with me. If you have a personal connection to a police officer, you can ask them, and they'll likely confirm that this is the truth. I will say, not everyone in that pre-shift huddle was excited about making arrests, and I was one of them. I was content with patrolling my area and responding to calls for service. However, in those moments of absolute calm, I might have indulged in some YouTube content.

Now, regarding the incident involving the officer who recklessly pursued the vehicle, one might expect that he faced severe consequences, including termination or legal repercussions. However, the reality was quite different. The officer received only a two-day suspension, a minimal punishment considering the gravity of the situation. Furthermore, he was allowed to choose which two days he wanted to serve his suspension.

By allowing him to choose which days he wished to serve his suspension it enabled him to ease the financial impact on his paycheck. But, if that wasn't surprising enough, this same officer in my opinion spit in the face of the deceased young lady when he went to the dispatch room and openly boasted to the dispatchers about receiving only a two-day suspension. This revelation left everyone, including those who were often regarded as problematic officers, utterly astonished. It was an outcome that nobody had anticipated. I distinctly recall discussing the matter with a sergeant who expressed his disbelief, mentioning that he believed that he would have been terminated for such an incident. This situation highlighted the unfortunate reality that true accountability in the police force was frequently applied selectively, mainly targeting the public while overlooking internal issues.

Off Duty Cop Punches a Lady in The Face

I also attempted to shed light on another deeply concerning incident that transpired within my department. During this particular incident, several officers decided to visit a local bar within the community, seeking an evening of relaxation, camaraderie, and, of course, drinks. As the night wore on, it became increasingly evident that these officers had indulged a bit too much, if not excessively.

Still under the influence of alcohol, a heated altercation suddenly erupted within the confines of the bar, escalating rapidly into a full-fledged brawl. What makes this situation particularly disturbing is the identity of those involved. It wasn't just ordinary citizens from the community caught up in this melee; it was also cops from the local police department.

It's a perplexing and rather concerning scenario when individuals who publicly profess to uphold higher standards and are expected to maintain law and order find themselves embroiled in a bar fight with members of the very community they are sworn to protect. However, the most distressing aspect of this incident is yet to be revealed.

In the midst of the chaos, one of the officers, who stands at approximately 6'5 and weighing around 240 pounds, deliberately aimed a devastating punch at a little petite lady's face. This punch landed with a powerful impact that knocked her unconscious. There was no doubt among those present, including fellow officers, that this act was far from accidental. You wouldn't believe that this incident quickly became a running joke that circulated throughout the department, even eliciting amusement from corporals, sergeants, lieutenants, and, shockingly, the chief.

Now, consider this: what do you think happened to this officer following such a grave transgression? Was he, for instance, arrested, fired, or perhaps suspended? The answer, astonishingly, was a mere suspension. But the duration of this suspension raises even more concerns. Yes, you guessed it, only two days. This two-day suspension thing was starting to become the norm when it came to disciplinary action from the Chief. What's more disturbing is he too was granted the privilege of selecting the specific two days for his suspension, minimizing the impact on his paycheck.

The justification provided for this lenient punishment was that the lady who had been knocked unconscious chose not to press charges against the officer. While on the surface, this decision may seem straightforward, but it leaves considerable room for speculation that there may have been more to the story than initially met the eye.

Cop Involved In 7 Shootouts

Another deeply troubling issue that I came across during my time as a police officer was the disturbing case of a fellow cop who had been involved in not one, not two, but seven separate police-related shootings with unarmed citizens. What made this situation even more perplexing was the leniency of the punishment meted out to this officer: a mere two-day suspension, regardless of the gravity of these incidents, or he was always cleared of any wrongdoing.

Unable to reconcile this apparent lack of accountability, I began asking questions about these incidents, and making multiple attempts to understand how this particular officer consistently managed to escape serious consequences after each of his alarming shootouts with unarmed individuals. It seemed only logical to seek clarity on this deeply concerning matter.

However, my attempts to shed light on this issue were met with resistance and disapproval from within the department. I was scolded on several occasions for daring to ask too many questions. The prevailing sentiment seemed to be that it was not my place to inquire about such matters and that I should refrain from meddling in affairs that were supposedly beyond my concern. This response left me profoundly perplexed and disheartened, as it seemed to imply that the pursuit of justice and accountability within our ranks was, at best, a secondary consideration.

Unfortunately, my quest for further information on the latter issue was met with resistance, which left me feeling as though I were navigating a dangerous path that I did not wish to tread any further on. While I never sensed I was in any personal danger, I was aware that my actions might jeopardize my job which I definitely needed at the time.

I began reading between the lines to discern that pushing further would only lead to more challenges that I could not overcome. Regrettably, my efforts to uncover what really happened concerning those incidents yielded no additional insights. However, one thing remained abundantly clear to me: a single individual held the authority to sanction such actions—our Chief. This realization allowed me to see the challenges that awaited individuals like me—those who had ventured into this career field with optimism and a degree of gullibility.

Chapter 8

The Mind of Cops

I firmly believe that one reason the mind of cops can be so prone to manipulation and indoctrination is due to the kind of individuals who typically become cops. This type of mindset often belongs to those who may never have held any significant authority in their lives prior to putting on the badge. As you guys have suspected, it's true that many cops have experienced some form of bullying at some point in their lives and believe it or not the bullying often continues within the police department itself.

Many cops harbor a certain level of fear when carrying out their duties, so when a cop says he or she fears for their life, take it seriously, it's not a mere exaggeration. You see, many cops join the force at a relatively young age, and they may not have encountered significant life challenges up to that point. They enter the police academy with limited life experience and from there they transition directly into the police department, sometimes even advancing to supervisory positions without significant mental growth throughout their careers.

Consequently, when members of the public seek to speak with supervisors in situations where their rights have been violated, they might find themselves facing someone with a similar mindset as the initial responding officer. These are often individuals who may have never experienced a real-world altercation before becoming a police officer, yet they are tasked with enforcing laws and managing potentially volatile situations. Certainly, the situation can be intimidating, especially for a younger police officer. It's crucial to remember that these officers are armed, and in moments of fear or heightened tension, they have, regrettably, resorted to the use of deadly force.

Since 2017, there have been a total of 6,767 instances in the United States where unarmed citizens were shot and tragically killed in encounters with police (source: Statista https://www.statista.com/statistics/585152/people-shot-to-death-by-us-police-by-race/). In contrast, during the same period, the number of police officers who lost their lives was 1,800 (source: The National Officers Memorial Fund https://nleomf.org/memorial/facts-figures/officer-fatality-data/officer-deaths-by-year/). It's important to note that not all of these police deaths were the result of interactions with citizens; some occurred in various other incidents.

When we examine these numbers in comparison, the discrepancy is striking. The significantly higher count of unarmed citizens who were shot and killed by police underlines the importance of de-escalation training, and a revamping of police academies as a whole.

Allow me to tell a quick story about one of the cops I used to work with. I once had a partner who carried himself as an authoritative individual with his deep voice and imposing presence, but, in reality, he was one of the most fearful cops I knew. His forceful character only surfaced when several other cops were present. When alone, his confidence would quickly fade. This was noticed on several different occasions.

One particular night, we were called to clear a house. Clearing a house, as a cop, is where we enter with our guns drawn to ensure there are no threats to ourselves or the citizens we're protecting. Sometimes, these situations unfold in pitch-black darkness, where the person or people inside could see us better than we can see them due to the poor lighting during late night hours. What makes it even more dangerous is the possibility of being illuminated by outside lights like streetlamps, making us visible to anyone inside.

One night, around 2 am, I was paired with this particular officer, except this time I couldn't hear the deep voice and his presence wasn't so big anymore. Despite his bold demeanor in the presence of other cops, he displayed an overwhelming fear. It was going to be my job to lead the way as we entered the home. However, his anxiety got the better of him, and he turned on his flashlight, shining it right on me, essentially giving away our position. I won't lie, for a moment, I questioned whether he was genuinely scared or attempting to set me up.

I firmly, and I do mean firmly, instructed him to turn off his light, and we tried again. Before proceeding, I glanced back at him, only to find his gun drawn, aimed towards my back, eyes wide with fear, him breathing heavily, and his hands trembling. I feared more for my life from him than the potential threat inside. With hands shaking the way his hands were shaking while holding a gun I was afraid he was going to shoot me in the back. I didn't have faith that I would be able to clear this home with him operating as my partner, I replaced him with another well-trained officer that I had more confidence in.

Now, it's vital to understand that everyone, including myself, experiences fear in these situations, but there's a critical difference between being afraid and letting fear control you, which this officer unfortunately did. This incident highlighted a pattern where he allowed fear to dictate his actions, despite portraying an entirely different demeanor while in the presence of several other cops.

In law enforcement, it's crucial to recognize that not all officers can relate to the challenges faced by the communities they serve. Many officers, like the one in this incident, may still live at home and lack real-life experiences that help them empathize with citizens. I want to make it clear that I'm not passing judgment on anyone for living with their parents. My intention is solely to emphasize my point. My point being it's easier to understand the issues that a member of the public may be dealing with if you have had to experience the same or similar issue yourself.

For example, I never issued citations for expired registrations because I understood the struggle firsthand. When I moved to Georgia, my wife and I faced a financial setback, making it impossible to afford our vehicle registrations. In Georgia, vehicle registration mandates a fee based on a percentage of the vehicle's worth. This could amount to several hundred or even thousands of dollars for the initial registration. I drove around with an expired registration for nearly a year, and my wife for even longer. Imagine that, while working as a cop I drove my personal vehicle with an expired registration myself. The reason behind this was, despite having a job, my paycheck hardly covered the expenses, which included bills, insurance, and trying to catch up on overdue payments.

Experiencing this situation allowed me to empathize with people who might not have had the financial means to renew their vehicle registrations. I would have felt like a real hypocrite if I had written a citation for an expired registration, knowing firsthand how challenging life could be at times. Writing a simple citation could further push someone into a financial hole they were already struggling to climb out of. Through this experience and others, I came to understand that police officers often police based on their own life experiences. If you have a cop who lacks life experience, has never held authority before, and has faced bullying both in and out of the department, this is the type of cop who can make life difficult for citizens.

Chapter 9

The Beginning of the End

So, when it all boiled down to it, I began to see that I was nothing like most of these guys that I worked with. I now faced a pivotal choice: stay with the department or leave. I weighed various factors, such as whether I needed the job (which was an unequivocal yes) and whether I wanted it (which was an unequivocal no). Reflecting on my career, I began to realize something significant. Despite entering this profession with lofty expectations and ultimately feeling let down, I discovered that I could still assist people in understanding their rights. However, I also understood that I didn't have to be part of a police department to do so.

At this point there have been several situations that made me question whether our presence was truly meant for public service or if it was merely a facade, aimed at deceiving the community into believing we had a positive image, all while we performed solely for the cameras. Before giving an example of what I am saying, allow me to first recount another experience during my time as a police officer. Despite the prior unsettling situations, this particular incident solidified the fact that our primary mission was not community service.

Do Good Cops Exist? Yes or No.

But before I proceed, I want to be fair and acknowledge that there are both good and bad cops. While some argue that there are no good cops, I beg to differ. I believe I was a good cop and I also believe there are many other good cops who may work for bad departments. However, I believe that good cops often have shorter careers because they recognize their own value and refuse to allow the department's system to exploit them any further.

Many members of the public often wonder, "If a cop is truly good, why didn't they report their corrupt colleague?" The truth is that many cops, including myself, have reported misconduct by fellow officers to their superiors. Unfortunately, this often leads to retaliation, bullying, threats to their job security, or even physical harm. Cops live in fear after taking a stand because it jeopardizes their livelihoods. When they do come forward, they find little support from anyone including the community. The lack of support from the community often stems from a lack of awareness about the events that have occurred.

A great example of what I mean is the case of Cariol Horne, a Buffalo, New York police officer who stopped another officer from choking a member of the public, only to lose her job and pension. She fought for 15 years to regain her pension, and it took a long time for justice to prevail. The worst part is that most people are unaware of this case and many like it. The media rarely covers these stories, and cops are often left to fend for themselves. I know of several stories similar to this one.

My point is that I don't agree with the claim that there are no good cops. I believe that when good cops act in the best interests of the people, their efforts are often concealed, and the public remains unaware of what truly transpires within the police force. Imagine how many cops have jeopardized their careers or left their jobs just to hear that there are no good cops, not even one.

Now imagine being that cop receiving death threats or struggling to make ends meet because you prioritized the public's welfare over your own, as cops are supposed to do. However, imagine doing all of this only to find out that your efforts go unnoticed. It's a lonely and terrifying place to be, with no one coming to the aid of these cops who are almost always hung out to dry.

Why do I bring up these issues now? I would like to walk you through my own departure from the police department. I encountered a situation very much like the one I just described, where I believed a member of the public was not only being exploited but was also about to be wrongly charged with a crime. I couldn't sit idly by and do nothing. Therefore, I made the tough decision to disregard direct orders, fully expecting to be fired that very night.

John's Arrest

So, what happened, you ask. I was near a neighborhood not far from the police department, where there was a four-way stop sign that drivers were notorious for disregarding. I started keeping a close watch on this intersection because I knew it was also a path that local children often took to reach the nearby store. One day, as I sat by the stop sign ensuring compliance, a group of young neighborhood kids walked by. In a playful mood, I struck up a conversation with them, and they informed me they were heading to the store to buy some candy. I jokingly asked them to bring me back some candy and other delicious treats. As they continued on their way, they laughed and carried on.

Upon their return, I engaged with them once more. Unfortunately, the kids didn't bring me any candy, although they kindly offered to share theirs. I declined graciously, joking that I was watching my figure at the time lol.

As the kids walked further away towards their homes, a car sped through the very same stop sign at what seemed like 35 mph, without ever touching its brakes. My immediate thought was just moments earlier, those kids had been crossing that intersection. What if they had still been crossing when that reckless driver sped through? They could have suffered serious injuries or even lost their lives due to the driver's thoughtless actions.

Without hesitation, I pursued the vehicle and attempted to initiate a traffic stop. Once behind the vehicle, I promptly informed dispatch of my location and reported that I was initiating a 10-38 with a red SUV. "10-38" is the police code that we used for conducting a traffic stop. Strangely, the vehicle didn't slow down, but it also wasn't attempting to evade me.

Again, I relayed the situation to dispatch, and my supervisor contacted me via the radio to gain more information about what was transpiring. This is the proper protocol, in contrast to the earlier example of the cop who falsely claimed not to be chasing but merely trying to catch up to a vehicle.

Here's how it should work: first, when you attempt to conduct a traffic stop and the vehicle refuses to stop, you inform dispatch and your supervisor (often, the supervisor initiates contact). Second, the supervisor would inquire about the reason for the traffic stop. If it's not for one of the serious offenses outlined in policy, the supervisor will instruct you to turn off your lights and sirens and pull over to the side of the road, ensuring that the driver you're trailing can see that you've ceased any further attempts to stop them.

This is done to avoid alarming the driver and potentially triggering a dangerous chase for minor offenses, as we learned earlier an incident like that could be tragic. Third, you allow the driver to drive out of sight, and you turn in the opposite direction. Again, the emphasis is on not engaging in pursuits that could pose greater risks to the public.

Just as I was about to turn around and end the encounter, I noticed the vehicle pulling into a McDonald's parking lot. Believing the driver had finally decided to stop, I followed and parked behind him. After completing all the necessary traffic stop procedures mentioned earlier on in "Chapter 5 Traffic Stop Basics", I approached the driver and inquired why he did not stop initially when I signaled him to do so. He was visibly nervous, and it soon became clear why. As he rolled down his window a bit further, I detected a strong odor of marijuana coming from the vehicle. It's important to note that this occurred before marijuana was being legalized in certain states.

As I continued the stop, I discovered that both his driver's license and registration were suspended, which is a misdemeanor in Georgia. Also, he had just technically eluded me when he failed to comply with my initial attempt to stop him. He also lacked insurance, and in Georgia, driving without insurance leads to vehicle towing. Not to mention I found more marijuana under his seat.

From this point forward, I'll refer to him as John. I learned that John had driven to McDonald's because it was his workplace, and he wanted to leave his vehicle in a safe spot, anticipating that he might be headed to jail. After further conversation, it became clear that John had accumulated too many violations to avoid arrest. While I typically looked for opportunities to issue citations instead of making an arrest, in this case, he had multiple infractions simultaneously. Therefore, I placed John under arrest and transported him to the police department for processing.

During the ride to the station, John and I engaged in a conversation that left a positive impression on me. He was genuinely a good person just making some regrettable choices. I offered him advice and stressed the importance of taking responsibility. I advised him that the judge he would be facing was well regarded for being fair. I couldn't predict the outcome of his case, but I encouraged him to be honest and accountable, believing it to be his best course of action.

After John was booked, some time passed—approximately two months—then I received a subpoena for court, which turned out to be for John's case. I was quite puzzled because it seemed unusually fast for this case to be scheduled. Typically, it would take at least four to five months before someone's court date would come up. This baffled me, so I started asking nearly everyone on my shift about it, including my Lieutenant and a respected traffic officer known for his knowledge. However, nobody could provide an explanation.

When the court date arrived, I inquired with a court staff member about why this particular case was on the docket so soon, but they couldn't provide any answers either.

Sitting in the courtroom, I listened as the judge went through his cases, eventually arriving at John's case. The judge called John's name three times, but there was no response. I must admit I was disappointed because I had hoped that John would show up and take responsibility for his actions, thereby putting these issues behind him. The judge then requested the arresting officer, and I responded. After he asked a few questions, I informed the judge that I knew where John worked. In response, the judge issued a warrant for John's arrest, and I left the courtroom.

Later that night, I went to the McDonald's where John worked, but he wasn't there. I advised his co-workers not to inform John that I had been looking for him, though we all knew what was likely to happen. Later, around 11:30 pm, myself and a couple of other officers returned to the McDonald's, and there was John. I was somewhat surprised since I believed his co-workers had told him about our earlier visit. I asked John if they had informed him that I had come to his job earlier looking for him, and he confirmed that they had. At that point, I started to wonder, as most guilty individuals would avoid a place where they knew the police might be waiting to apprehend them. After stepping outside to speak with John, I asked him why he hadn't shown up for court. He looked at me suspiciously and replied, "I don't have to be in court until April." It's important to note that at that time the present date was February 14th.

Now thoroughly perplexed, I began to ask more questions of the officers who were on scene, as I had also found it strange that his case had been scheduled so soon, I asked John multiple times to confirm that he had the right court date. He assured me that he was certain and even offered to prove it. He asked if he could use my phone to call his wife and have her send a picture of the documents with his court date on it. I allowed him to use my phone because I wanted to ascertain the truth.

After speaking with John's wife, she texted over a picture of the documents, and indeed, there was an April 16th court date with my name on them indicating I was the arresting officer. It all started to make sense at that point—the court had made an error. I contacted my Lieutenant to explain the situation, but his response was not what I had hoped for. Due to the judge issuing a warrant, he advised me to arrest John anyway and bring him to the station to book him, suggesting that John could address the matter when he saw the judge. However, it was Friday night, and John had told me that he couldn't afford to go to jail because he was starting a new job at Walmart the next day.

Think about this: all of the charges against John likely stemmed from his inability to pay certain fines and fees, which was likely the reason he didn't have a valid license in the first place, that and maybe along with some other not so smart choices. I had encouraged him to take responsibility and work his way out of this situation. John had not only continued working at McDonald's but had also secured a second job at Walmart, acting on the advice I had given him. Now I was being ordered to disregard all of that and place him back in a difficult situation where he might not be able to escape. McDonald's might fire him for causing the police to show up for a second time, and Walmart could terminate him for missing his first day of work due to being in jail. This would push John further into the hole he was trying to climb out of. While my Lieutenant didn't seem too concerned about these repercussions, I certainly was.

As I drove John back to the police station, I was weighed down by the possibility of further complicating someone's life. When we arrived at the station, I took John into booking and had him sit at the desk directly in front of me. I did not proceed with booking him; instead, I sat there for about 20 minutes, contemplating. Eventually, I called my Sergeant, who was a step below the Lieutenant, and explained the entire situation. He, too, understood that this was not a good scenario.

I must add quickly that this particular Sergeant was undoubtedly the best in the department. He was supportive, despite his tough exterior. I believed he had also been unfairly passed over for promotions that he rightfully deserved. It seemed as if the good cops did not rise to the top in these types of departments. I just wanted to include that small bit.

The Sergeant then had me double, triple, and quadruple-check the documentation at the station to confirm beyond any doubt that April 16th was indeed the correct date. Once we were absolutely certain that John's court date wasn't until April, the Sergeant instructed me to call the judge. It was approximately 1 am at this point, and I was nervous because I had no idea how the judge would react. I wasn't sure if he would be angry and report me to the Chief or if he would listen. Given that I was already defying the Lieutenant's orders, I was quite anxious.

Finally, I dialed the judge's number, and he answered. "Hello, Judge," I said, and proceeded to explain everything, mirroring the conversation I had just had with my Sergeant. After a brief pause, the judge surprised me by instructing me to release John. My response was an immediate "Yes, sir." To my astonishment, he commended my actions, stating that I had done a good job. I hadn't anticipated such a response.

After hanging up the phone, I sat back in my seat for a moment and took a deep breath. I glanced over at John, who had tears in his eyes, as he stated, "I have never seen a cop fight to get someone out of jail before". Trying to hold back my own emotions, I told him, "None of this is your fault, and you don't deserve this. I wouldn't want to spend a second in jail for something I didn't do either."

I then made another call, this time to my Sergeant, to deliver the news. The Sergeant then instructed me to contact the Lieutenant. Another tough phone call awaited me. I called the Lieutenant and explained the situation, making it clear that the judge had ordered John's release.

Upon hearing this, the Lieutenant ordered John's release and suggested he take a Lyft back to work. However, I had reservations about this order as well. The way I saw it, the last time John's manager saw him, he was being led out of their establishment in handcuffs. It seemed inevitable that he would be fired upon his return to work. So, once again, I found myself disobeying a direct order. I placed John back in my car, drove him to McDonald's, and walked him inside. I explained to his managers that John hadn't done anything wrong, and this was a mix-up involving the department and the court. I emphasized that there was no longer a warrant for his arrest, and none of this should have happened.

Upon leaving, John walked me outside, and I encouraged him not to let this incident go unanswered. I suggested that he might have a case and should consider seeking legal counsel. John expressed relief that it was all over and said, "I just want to go to work and I'm happy not to be in jail for something I didn't do." While I respected his decision, I hoped he would follow up.

Sometime later, my wife and I were at Walmart, and John approached me. We struck up a conversation, and he walked us to our car; seeming to be in a better place emotionally, we exchanged phone numbers to stay in touch. To this day, we still check in on each other from time to time. When we left, my wife asked, "who was that", and I told her, "Remember the story about the guy who didn't stop at the stop sign? That was him." Her face lit up with recognition.

Chapter 10

The Downfall

I believe incidents like these are why we become police officers. We are meant to do what's right to the best of our knowledge and ability. These are the actions that restore the public's faith in those who wear the badge. Unfortunately, this wasn't the end of the story.

Towards the end of the shift, we all gathered in the patrol room for debriefing. I stood somewhat isolated, bracing myself for what the Lieutenant might say. He walked in, holding a cup of coffee and keeping his comments brief. He scanned the room but avoided eye contact with me until he reached my vicinity. Then, he stopped directly in front of me and said, "You did a good job", then he walked away. Once again, I was taken aback by this response. I quickly concluded my debrief and headed home, not allowing him the opportunity to change his mind or say anything further.

At this point, I had a false sense of accomplishment. I believed that maybe this could be the turning point that the department needed. I was engaging in wishful thinking, unaware of how others truly felt. I thought everything had worked out, but little did I know that this situation would resurface later.

Choosing Between Being a Father or a Cop

One day, as I laid in my bed preparing for my night shift, my kids, aged 5 and 6 at the time, along with my 8-year-old nephew, were playing in our front yard. My 26-year-old niece was with them keeping an eye on them. While I slept, I suddenly heard the terrifying screams of my children. I jumped out of my bed, feeling as though I couldn't move any faster than slow motion. In desperation my goal was to reach my children and find out why they were screaming in fear.

As I swung open the front door, I witnessed the neighbor's Doberman Pinscher chasing my children around our yard. Thank God my niece was with them because my five-year-old daughter, driven by fear, had ran in the opposite direction of our home. However, my niece reacted swiftly, grabbing her and both of them sought refuge atop our car.

The garage door was still open at this point, due to my son and nephew who had taken shelter inside of the house and they had forgotten to close it. At this time the dog had ceased its chase once everyone was safely out of reach. He then slowly started making his way toward my garage. If it had continued, it could have entered my home. I grabbed my firearm and called for the neighbors to come and retrieve their dog.

For those who might assume the dog simply wanted to play, I'll add some context. My neighbor's dogs had previously chased other neighbors and even bitten a woman living a few houses down from us. They were undeniably vicious and had a history of aggression. There was no indication that these dogs had any friendly intentions based on their past behavior. Many neighbors had already contacted the sheriff's department concerning the dogs, as it was not our jurisdiction. Our neighbors were known for using their dogs as tools of intimidation. This was an elderly couple, likely in their late 60s, who had no children and didn't allow anyone to visit their home.

When we first purchased the home, the neighbors were friendly but that changed into a bitter relationship very quickly. Initially, I believed our issues with the neighbors stemmed from my profession as a police officer, assuming they didn't like cops. However, I quickly learned that being a cop had nothing to do with it. They had conflicts with everyone in the neighborhood and had a notorious reputation for instigating disputes. You wouldn't expect someone of their age to be so contentious, but that was the reality. This issue existed even before we moved into the neighborhood, and to this day, people I stay in touch with who still live there report ongoing troubles caused by these neighbors.

As I mentioned, I grabbed my firearm and called for the neighbors to retrieve their dog. To my surprise, when I looked over, I saw the wife standing beside her house, merely observing the situation. She showed no urgency to come and get her dog until I threatened to shoot it. As she finally took her dog away, we exchanged heated words. I was extremely angry that she had allowed her dog to come into my yard and chase my children. I told her that my children would not be afraid to play in their own yard due to her dogs repeatedly jumping over the fence to chase them.

When I got to work that night, I filed a report with my shift supervisors, recounting everything that had happened. I made it clear to my supervisors that I would prioritize being a parent and protector of my children over being a police officer. After all, you can't reasonably expect someone to help protect the community if they won't even protect their own home, can you? Unfortunately, that was precisely what the department expected of me.

About six months later, I moved out of the house and turned it over to my parents. I feared that one day those dogs might attack my children when I wasn't around, and even my response to the situation might not have been enough to prevent a tragic outcome. I relocated to an apartment until we could purchase another home. I still took my children over to the home to play with their cousin, but I always sat outside with them while they played to ensure their safety.

While sitting outside one day, I noticed that the husband was recording my children from a bedroom upstairs in their home. Shortly after, I observed the wife coming outside with their dogs. It appeared that they only ventured outside when the children were playing. On this day, I decided to observe them closely, and I think I finally understood their motives. Their disdain had nothing to do with my profession as a cop, and it wasn't related to race, as they were an interracial couple. It had nothing to do with any personal grievances against me; rather, it seemed to be triggered by the sounds of children playing.

They only seemed to emerge and engage in their disruptive behavior when the children were active. I had finally cracked the code. The only thing I couldn't fathom was why they disliked children. I could only speculate that it had something to do with the noise children naturally make. What was clear to me was that anyone who harbors such hatred for children must have experienced some deeply troubling past situation or perhaps had ongoing mental health issues.

While I sat pondering these revelations, the wife, who I will not name for legal reasons at this moment, brought the dogs outside. I discreetly began recording her actions, and she remained unaware that I was inside my vehicle, observing the scene unfold through its tinted windows. I captured footage of her bringing her sizable dog near the fence where my daughter was riding her scooter. When the dog got close enough, it lunged toward the fence.

At this point, I couldn't tolerate them using their dogs as an intimidation tool any longer. I jumped out of my vehicle and shouted at her, I must confess that I wasn't Officer Abiyah Israel in that moment; I was Abiyah Israel, the concerned parent who felt that his neighbors were intentionally endangering the safety of his children.

Remember, their dog had already jumped over our fence and chased my children around our yard. Moreover, while this was happening, the wife had merely observed without making any effort to restrain her dog. Now, the dog was lunging toward the fence to get closer to my daughter and I fully believed the dog was able to come over the fence yet again. I rushed over and the neighbor and I exchanged heated words. People often ask me what I feel like I did wrong as a cop, well, if you want to count this situation as something that I did wrong, then that's fine. But I was acting as a parent, not a cop, and at that point, I had had enough. I won't repeat the words that were exchanged between us, but we were both shouting at each other very loudly.

I made sure to file another incident report with the sheriff's office to document the incident because it was evident that my own department would not take any action. About three months after this incident, I received a call from the captain informing me that I would be under investigation by Internal Affairs, and he explained the reason why. I was somewhat surprised because I had not broken any laws, and I had reported this incident multiple times by that point. Furthermore, I had both video footage and photographs as evidence.

I have added a couple of those pictures of the husband standing at the fence with one of their dogs trying to intimidate our children. You could hear the dog growl whenever the kids ran by too fast. You can also see my nephew nonchalantly walking on our property and not even looking their way. I instructed all the children to act as if they weren't aware of the neighbor's actions. One would think that after so long, a person would stop and just go about their business, but they persisted, with these occurrences happening at least twice a week. Again, I remain clueless as to why they held such animosity toward children.

Although these neighbors were a nuisance, I couldn't stop them, they were on their property, but it just goes to show the mindset and intentions of the individual in these pictures.

The neighbor making his dog stare at our children attempting to scare them.

Suddenly, I found myself facing an Internal Affairs (IA) investigation, and the reason for it was my argument with the neighbor. She claimed that I had threatened to shoot her dog if it ever set foot on my property again. When the captain inquired about this, I responded that if any of those dogs posed a threat to me or my children, whether on my property or off it, I would defend myself and my children. So, would I shoot the dogs if necessary? Yes, I would. I believed that neither I nor my children should be afraid to walk around on our own property. Also, according to state law, I had every right to defend myself and my children.

Universal Citation: GA Code § 16-3-21 (2020)

    a. *A person is justified in threatening* or using force against another when and to the extent that he or she reasonably believes that such threat or force is necessary to defend himself or herself or a third person against such other's imminent use of unlawful force; however, except as provided in Code Section 16-3-23, a person is justified in using force which is intended or likely to cause death or great bodily harm only if he or she reasonably believes that such force is necessary to prevent death or great bodily injury to himself or herself or a third person or to prevent the commission of a forcible felony.

At the conclusion of the IA investigation, there was no wrongdoing found on my part. Even though I was cleared legally but according to the department I acted unbecoming of an officer. Therefore, I was asked to apologize, to which I intensely refused. Not only that, but I was also told I would be demoted from FTO, serve a two-week suspension without pay, and I would not be able to go up for promotion again. My reason for standing strong against apologizing to someone who had repeatedly placed my children in danger was due to knowing much of the department's history when it came to disciplining cops.

Knowing this caused me to questioned whether the chief required the officer who killed a young girl to apologize for his actions, or the officer who had punched a young lady in the face during a bar fight, knocking her out cold, or the two officers who tried to kill one another in the patrol room, or even the cop who was caught driving under the influence by his own department, the department I now worked for.

So, a little about that situation. After he, the cop who worked for our department was stopped for DUI, he initially pulled over to the side of the road before leading several cops on a high-speed chase or a 10-80 through the city. However, this cop was eventually caught and fired but surprisingly he was later rehired and promoted after two years. Why then was I facing more severe consequences for a statement made in defense of my children, a statement which was backed by the laws of the state of Georgia, and supported by photo and video evidence?

The question remained: why was my punishment so much harsher than that given to other officers in the department? Keep in mind all the details presented in this book. I had never fully conformed to the department's expectations. Moreover, I had recently helped a person to be released from jail, a person who I had now become friends with. While on the surface I was commended for my actions concerning that incident, secretly it seemed that they truly did not like my efforts, and they were simply waiting for me to slip up.

Therefore, I must admit that I may have given them the opportunity they were waiting for. Up to this point, my record as a police officer was pristine, with no complaints from any member of the public, not even one. Yet now the Chief wanted to impose severe penalties on me because I stated my intentions to protect my children. I knew this was all a message from the Thin blue Line as I came to know them, and it killed two birds with one stone. I'm sure they felt that they would have been able to teach me a lesson about loyalty, hang me out to dry again, and use me as an example to show that the chief holds his officers accountable.

Chapter 11

Looking Good for The Camera

Earlier, I mentioned that we weren't there to truly help the community but rather to look good for the cameras. Let me explain further. All of this transpired in 2020, during the widespread riots in the US following the events surrounding George Floyd. The riots were spreading, and the department's goal at the time was to present itself as prestigious as possible. News cameras were all around and all the officers had to play the role. Previous incidents involving department officers had already been discreetly addressed, with minor punishments like two-day suspensions and reassignments. With that being said the hypocrisy couldn't get any worse, the Chief was now organizing an event at the police department called "Cops for Accountability." This too was a facade aimed at improving the department's public image and looking good in front of the cameras.

In Chapter 4 concerning the Chief, I mentioned two situations where it seemed that his main concern was preserving the department's reputation rather than addressing significant internal issues or steering the department toward genuine accountability. This is one of the situations I was referring to. He seemed to turn a blind eye to the department's serious violations. However, when the media came knocking for interviews, he put on a facade of a chief who holds his officers accountable. I believe that the two-week suspension, demotion, apology, and other punishments they attempted to impose on me should have been directed at the officers who truly deserved them.

I now understand that this is how things operate in such departments. If you don't conform to the way they want you to play the game, don't expect them to come to your aid. Sound familiar? Now, I faced a difficult decision. It was either I accept the suspension, demotion, and the agreement that I could not be promoted again, and issue an apology, or I leave the department. I made my choice; I chose to become a full-time parent. There was no way I could continue working for a department that seemed eager and ready to take any opportunity to harm my career, simply because I wanted to be the police officer, I initially signed up to be.

I wish I could have continued my service because I genuinely enjoyed my job, and I was aware that the community I served appreciated my efforts. The fact that I had never received a single complaint from the general public during my years of service indicated to me that I was on the right track. My issues were primarily with the corrupt mentality and the lack of accountability within the police department. The Chief's hypocrisy had become unbearable, and I could no longer tolerate it. It was a choice between leaving on my own terms or eventually facing termination because I refused to play their game.

Chapter 12

What's Next for Me?

I didn't have a clear plan, but I knew I wanted to leverage what I had learned in law enforcement. I wanted a career where I could earn a living, have peace of mind, and continue helping people. One day, my wife suggested that I teach people about their basic rights. Not just teach them but make the learning process easy and enjoyable. I thought this was a fantastic idea, so I started exploring how to get started. In my YouTube video, "Good Cop Leaves Police Force | What They Told Me To Do To Citizens!" where I explained why I left the department, I mentioned that during one of those slow nights when there was nothing to do, I was watching YouTube and stumbled upon the YouTube Channel "Big Nick South Florida Accountability." This was my introduction to the Auditing Community and actually finding out what auditors were. From there, I watched other channels covering 1A Audits, and I shared this interest with my friends.

One of my friends suggested that I do a video review and share my online course as well. I decided to give it a shot. I made a video and it only had 7 views in 6 days. I thought nothing of it, I just continued to think about my plans for the future and YouTube wasn't really a part of it. However, on day 7 the video took off! That video ended up getting well over 1 million views, and from that point onward, I started receiving tons messages and videos to review.

I won't deny that this entire process became overwhelming. I couldn't keep up with the influx of emails and the comments that flooded the comment sections of videos. People sometimes forget that I'm just one person, and it's impossible for me to see and respond to them all. Nevertheless, I found myself deeply involved in a community I had never imagined. It felt like my prayers had been answered. I could now teach basic rights, make a living, and not worry about corruption. However, I soon realized that no place is perfect, and I began to discover flaws even in this new endeavor.

When I said I wanted to help people, I genuinely meant it. I'm not perfect, nor do I possess all knowledge, but I started to notice that some in this community were solely motivated by money. While I believe people should be compensated for their work, prioritizing money above all else in this niche is problematic. For instance, I received videos from viewers, and while they might have made for sensational content and garnered many views, it's essential to maintain a conscience while doing what we do. We must understand that if we're not honest in our opinions about these situations, viewers and followers could adopt those false opinions, believe they are right, and potentially take actions based on inaccurate information, which could lead to detentions, arrests, or worse outcomes.

I'll clarify my stance so that you understand my point clearly. I once received a video from a woman in Georgia, she wanted me to review and share it. After watching the video and reviewing the laws, I advised her that the police were actually right in this instance, and she was actually in violation of Georgia state law. I didn't want to cover the video and give her a false impression that her actions were correct. This could lead her to believe that she could always respond in this manner, potentially landing her in trouble or worse. So, I chose to be honest with her, even though she didn't like my response.

However, she sent the video to another channel, and that channel covered it, presenting it as if the police were wrong in this particular case. While it's true that the police are wrong quite often, in this instance, they were right. Giving the viewer a false sense of being right can ultimately hurt her and anyone else who watches that video. They may believe her actions were correct and then attempt to repeat them, but it may not work out in their favor. While I understand that some actually make a living through auditing and covering audits, it should not come at the expense of possibly misleading people and putting them in harm's way. So, please know that if I don't believe something is correct, I will say so, as money is not more important than honesty and safety.

Another situation I encountered in this community involved a video I was asked to review. I thought the person who sent the video was one of the individuals in the video, but I later found out that this was not the case. Subsequently, I received a copyright strike, the first for my channel, from Justin Pulliam. I was taken aback by this, and I reached out to him to explain that I thought it was ok to share and I could take the video down. I let him know there was no need to report my channel to YouTube. Unfortunately, he chose to ignore me.

I must take responsibility for this because I should have been more cautious and not rushed to cover a video without properly vetting the person who sent it. However, when you receive a high volume of emails, it can be overwhelming at times. What surprised me the most was that this same individual regularly covers other people's videos but filed a copyright strike against my channel for covering his video, something he does routinely. Nonetheless, I accept the blame for this situation, although it does strike me as somewhat hypocritical and seems to be centered around competition and money.

With that being said, I want to take a moment to thank channels like **Direct D**, who was the first to reach out and assist me in comprehending various aspects of the auding community that I was unaware of. He played a crucial role in broadening my perspective by introducing me to valuable insights I hadn't previously considered.

Also, **San Joaquin Valley Transparency** deserves a ton of recognition for dedicating his time to help guide me on navigating the YouTube system and helping to address the challenges that arose when I was effortlessly trying to educate people about their rights.

I'd also like to extend my gratitude to **Big Nick South Florida Accountability**, who became a true friend during a period when I truly needed one. He regularly reached out to inquire about my well-being, and that gesture meant more to me than he could possibly realize. We have made several plans, and I am looking forward to working with one of the best auditors on YouTube, Big Nick!

Finally, I'd like to express my appreciation to **LackLuster** for also aiding me in navigating YouTube, especially during times when I believed my channel was being targeted for cancellation. He consistently offered his assistance to the best of his ability, and for that, I'm thankful my friend.

I'd also like to extend my gratitude to anyone else who has provided me with valuable insights into YouTube and the auditing community. I still consider myself a learner in this space. So, once again, I want to say thank you to those channels for all their support.

I also want to extend a huge thank you to the We the People University viewers who have subscribed, joined the channel, purchased merchandise, bought the app and the course. Your support means the world to me, and I appreciate you holding me accountable when I make mistakes. Finally, I must thank God for leading me out of that mentally corrupt department and allowing me to find a position where I truly love what I do now.

In conclusion, after dealing with scare tactics, food bribes to write more citations, dishonesty, a lack of accountability, and brainwashing in the police department, I'm genuinely happy to be here with you all. I hope that by reading this book, some of the questions you had for me have been answered. I plan to do live streams soon so we can have more interactive discussions because you are the reason, I'm doing what I do. Thank you, and may God bless you all!

Captain Ed

I understand that many people due to reading this book thus far, might assume that the entire police department lacked good officers, but that's not the case. I want to highlight one individual who stood out to me as someone who genuinely cared about the well-being of not just police officers but people. One day during our Emergency Vehicle Operators Course (EVOC) training, our group took a lunch break. We headed to a nearby restaurant close to the training grounds. As we entered the restaurant, all the seats quickly filled up, leaving me without a spot to sit. This situation didn't bother me, as I had already mentioned that I preferred not to be around many of them anyway. Their seating arrangement inadvertently allowed me to find a seat away from the group. Besides I've always been comfortable being alone.

While I was eating, one of the captains, who was a lieutenant at the time, glanced over at me. His facial expression showed that of genuine concern at the fact that I was sitting alone. I observed as he left his seat among the other officers, grabbed his tray of food, and came over to sit with me. He said, "There is no way I'm going to let my guy sit by himself." When he mentioned "my guy," he wasn't using it in a professional context implying that I worked for him; it was more of an informal and friendly term. Even though I was content with sitting alone, his gesture showed me that he cared not only for police officers but for people in general. This perception of him was reinforced by his interactions with the public.

Most higher-level supervisors didn't often patrol the streets or conduct traffic stops, but occasionally, the chief and the command staff joined us lower-level officers on the street to show unity, I guess. During one of these instances, I had the opportunity to witness this captain, Captain Ed, in action. He was one of the most polite police officers you would ever encounter. Believe it or not, he had a unique way of handling situations that could even make the angriest driver smile about receiving a citation.

Watching him interact with a member of the public during a traffic stop taught me a lot. I started modeling my own approach to traffic stops after his example. Not only did I take notes and learn valuable lessons in dealing with the public, but I also witnessed a good cop treating everyone with the respect they deserved. This wasn't a one-time occurrence; he consistently treated everyone the same way. I wouldn't want to miss the opportunity to express my gratitude to him for his fair treatment and for being an outstanding person overall. Thank you, Captain Ed, and congratulations on your promotion.

It is important to understand that there are actions you can take to ensure that your interactions with law enforcement remain within legal bounds and do not escalate. Being knowledgeable about your rights and the procedures used by law enforcement can greatly enhance the likelihood of a peaceful outcome.

THE 10 RULES TO REMEMBER WHEN DEALING WITH THE POLICE:

1. REMEMBERING YOUR RIGHTS: It is important to be aware of your constitutional rights, such as the right to remain silent, the right to an attorney, and the right to not consent to a search without a warrant. Knowing your rights and understanding how to exercise them can help protect you during interactions with the police.

2. STAYING CALM: Keeping a calm demeanor during interactions with the police can help to avoid escalating a situation and potentially dangerous confrontation.

3. NOT CONSENTING TO A SEARCH: Unless the police have a warrant or there are exigent circumstances, you have the right to not consent to a search of your person, property, or belongings.

4. ASKING FOR A WARRANT: If the police request to search your property, it is important to ask if they have a warrant. If they do not have a warrant, you have the right to not consent to the search.

5. REFRAINING FROM CONFESSING: It is important to remain silent and not confess to any allegations made against you. Anything you say can and will be used against you in a court of law.

6. AVOIDING PHYSICAL CONTACT: It is important to avoid physically touching or
putting the officer in fear. Physical confrontations can escalate the situation and put you in danger.

7. REMAINING SILENT: You have the right to remain silent and not incriminate yourself. Exercising this right can protect you during interactions with the police.

8. ASKING IF YOU ARE FREE TO GO: If you are being detained, it is important to ask if you are free to go. If you are not being arrested, the police should allow you to leave.

9. REQUESTING AN ATTORNEY: If you are being arrested, you have the right to an attorney. It is important to exercise this right and request an attorney to represent you.

10. FILING A COMPLAINT: If you believe your rights were violated during an interaction with the police, it is important to file a complaint. This can help hold the police accountable and prevent similar incidents from happening in the future.

Search and Seizure: Law enforcement is allowed to conduct searches and seizures without a warrant in specific reasonable situations. However, it's important to note that if a police officer tries to search you or your property without meeting one of the following conditions, they would be infringing upon your rights.

1. **Consent**: If the police ask you for your consent to search your home, car, or belongings, YOU MAY REFUSE. If you freely and voluntarily give the police your consent to search you or your property, the police are allowed to search without probable cause. You can always withdraw your consent if the cop has not found anything that would give him probable cause to continue searching. Many people give consent to search their house, car, or other belongings because they believe they must. Don't make that mistake! Consent induced by a threat or promise of a benefit or reward is generally not voluntary and will invalidate the subsequent search. For example, if an officer is at your house and says they're going to call the *Department of Family and Child Services* to take custody of a child if you don't consent, any consent under that circumstance is invalid and can be challenged.

2. **Plain View**: Officers do not need a warrant to seize illegal contraband if they observe it from a legal vantage point. Example: If you pull into a parking space and a police officer that is standing on the sidewalk notices drugs on your passenger seat, he has not searched your car because the items are in

"plain view." He can likely seize them and may have probable cause to make an arrest and conduct a full search of your car. Similarly, evidence may be in plain view if it is in your yard or in an open field, even if that area is part of your property.

3. **Stop & Frisk**: If you are suspected of possibly committing a crime the police can stop you if you are walking, driving, biking, or boating. The only thing that is needed is Reasonable Articulable Suspicion (RAS) that you have, or about to, or are in the process of committing a crime.

    - Police may stop you to ask questions and may frisk you for concealed weapons if they reasonably believe you are armed.

    - Under the 1968 landmark case of **Terry v. Ohio,** the U.S. Supreme Court ruled that it is not unconstitutional for police to "stop and frisk" a person if they reasonably suspect them to be armed and involved in a crime. This is strictly limited to the scope of pat-downs for items that are likely to be weapons. However, under more recent decisions, if an officer finds contraband during the pat-down, he is allowed to seize it. This is called "plain feel" and is like plain view. To conduct an investigatory stop, a police officer must have a reasonable, articulable suspicion that criminal activity has or is about to occur. Articulable suspicion is an easier standard for an officer to meet than probable cause but must still be supported by objective evidence. So, remember this: Investigatory stops require only a reasonable (articulable) suspicion, while arrests require probable cause or a warrant.

4. **Hot Pursuit**: If someone commits a crime and then tries to escape, the police in the pursuit are allowed to search the area to which that person runs. They may search this area for weapons the suspect might use, contraband which they have concealed, abandoned, or might destroy, or people who could help the criminal to escape.

5. In An Emergency: In the landmark case of **Carroll v. the U.S.**, a 1925 U.S. Supreme Court case, the court first established what is referred to as "the automobile exception" to the 4th Amendment. Because automobiles can be easily moved and their contents easily removed, police possessing probable cause that a crime is being committed may stop and search vehicles without warrants. Likewise, if the police reasonably believe that they must take immediate action to protect life or property, they may conduct a search. In such circumstances, referred to as "exigent circumstances" they are allowed to seize evidence – but only if it is likely to be destroyed or removed before they can obtain a warrant.

6. **As Part of An Arrest**: (Incident to Arrest)- Under most circumstances, police may search you and the area in your immediate control as part of a lawful arrest. This is referred to as a "search incident to arrest. However, not all arrests are lawful, and you may be able to challenge a warrantless search conducted after an unlawful arrest.

7. **Michigan Dept. of State Police v. Sitz** was a United States Supreme Court case involving the constitutionality of police sobriety checkpoints. The Court held 6-3 that these checkpoints met the Fourth Amendment standard of "reasonable search and seizure".

8. **DUI** - If an officer detects the odor of alcohol or marijuana or observes other manifestations of impairment (such as bloodshot or glassy eyes or slurred speech) during such a checkpoint, he may require you to submit to field sobriety tests to determine if you are driving under the influence of alcohol, drugs, or a combination of the two. If you are arrested because of these tests, your vehicle will likely be impounded and its contents searched, a procedure called "impound and inventory." You are under no legal requirements to take a Field Sobriety Test. Remember to read all state laws that are relevant to your state concerning this matter. Refusal of chemical or blood test could result in the suspension of your driver license.

    • The Supreme Court has also ruled that law enforcement agencies can use roadblocks to help solve specific crimes. For example, in ***Illinois v. Lidster***, the Court held that a police checkpoint for the purpose of gaining information about a hit-and-run accident that occurred at the same location and time of night as the checkpoint was a permissible activity.

   1. It is important to note that state constitutions may have stricter search and seizure rules than the federal Constitution, thus certain states might not allow roadblocks even in the situations outlined above. Remember that state constitutions can't offer less protection for state citizens than the federal Constitution, but they can offer more. For example, several states have prohibited drunk-driving checkpoints based on their state constitution.

9. **Police Dogs:** Police may generally use drug-sniffing dogs to detect the presence of narcotics without a warrant. Public places such as airports, bus terminals, and highways are commonly approved for "free air sniffs" by K-9s. However, a warrant is required if the dog physically intrudes upon a place where you have a reasonable expectation of privacy, such as your home. The U.S. Supreme Court ruled recently in Florida v. Jardines that the

use of a drug dog on the front porch of a home constitutes a search and therefore requires a warrant.

- The U.S. Supreme Court decided in the 2005 case of **Illinois v. Caballes**. Thus, the use of a trained detection dog does not require a warrant for the area around your vehicle.

- **Mapp v. Ohio**, 367 U.S. 643 (1961), was a landmark decision of the U.S. Supreme Court in which the Court ruled that the exclusionary rule, which prevents prosecutors from using evidence in court that was obtained by violating the Fourth Amendment to the U.S. Constitution.

You Have Been Arrested

1. Do not start talking. You have the right to remain silent. Tell the officer I am invoking my Fifth Amendment Right and "I would like to remain silent."
2. Do not answer any questions except your name, address, and date of birth.
3. Ask for a lawyer immediately. Be specific in your request for an attorney. Remain silent until you get an attorney. Remember what you say or do can and will be used against you in court.
    a. **Miranda v. Arizona**, 384 U.S. 436 (1966), was a landmark decision of the U.S. Supreme Court in which the Court ruled that the Fifth Amendment to the U.S. Constitution restricts prosecutors from using a person's statements made in response to interrogation in police custody as evidence at their trial unless they can show that the person was informed of the right to consult with an attorney before and during questioning, and of the right against self-incrimination before police questioning, and that the defendant not only understood these rights, but voluntarily waived them.
4. Remember anything you say when arrested, even if it's simple conversation in the back of the patrol car or once you are in jail, can be used against you. Other than basic identification information you have the right to wait to talk to a lawyer about any concern you may have with your arrest.

5. Even if you have not been read your rights at the scene when you encountered the police, anything you say or do will be used against you in court.

Miranda Rights

You have the right to remain silent. Anything you say can and will be used against you in a court of law. You have the right to an attorney. If you cannot afford an attorney, one will be appointed for you.

This indicates that you have the option to decline answering an officer's questions and can ask for an attorney. In case your rights have been infringed upon, regardless of whether you've been arrested, it's crucial to document the incident comprehensively. Compile information such as the officer's name and badge number, specify the particular right or rights violated, explain how they were violated, note the time, date, and location of the encounter, record the reason for the interaction, assess the officer's mood and tone, and check for potential witnesses. Ensure you gather anything else that can support the evidence of your rights being violated. Additionally, always remember to **CONTINUOUSLY RECORD POLICE** interactions!

Auditing Tips

I have been asked many times about best practices while auditing. There's no denying the number of auditors is growing by the day. So, what's causing the surge in auditors? I believe it's definitely a reflection of the current state of policing in America.

The main goal of auditing is to emphasize and reiterate that unless a law is broken, police have absolutely no authority over any citizen. Simply put, if you have not violated any law, you're entitled to exercise your fundamental rights freely. Another point of this movement is to raise awareness about our rights and teach individuals on how to assert them appropriately.

The primary thing I'd stress for auditors is the importance of maintaining composure. From my observations, successful audits are often those where the auditor remains calm and collected. I've witnessed audits that were loud and disruptive, these types of behaviors overshadow the main objective. It's crucial to remember that the primary goal is to enlighten, not to shock or entertain. When auditors adopt a confrontational stance, it detracts from the learning experience for all involved.

For those truly dedicated to the cause, remember educating should always take precedence. We must remember a significant number of people are still unaware of how to rightfully act when encountering the police, it is up to us to teach them.

Maintain Composure During Audits

Maintaining your calm during an audit not only ensures the process goes smoothly but also presents you in a favorable light. Overreacting or being confrontational often backfires, shifting negative attention towards the auditor rather than the subject of the audit. It's worth noting that even devoted followers of auditing videos can find obnoxious auditors off-putting. This sentiment isn't just mine, but I have read it in numerous comments and emails that I've come across. A composed demeanor not only reinforces the educational intent of the audit but also positions you as the rational party, which can be especially beneficial in legal situations.

Understand Your State Laws

It's alarming how many individuals that I have seen in a number of videos that are misinformed about their state laws. Relying solely on YouTube for legal information is a bit risky. While YouTube can be a valuable resource, it's no substitute for direct knowledge from legitimate state sources themselves. It's imperative that you study your state laws to ensure you're not accidentally violating any regulations during an audit. Being well-versed in your rights and obligations ensures you remain authoritative and credible during the auditing process.

Compliance with Legal Requirements is Crucial

One persistent issue I often observe in many videos is the lack of awareness or misunderstanding of case law like Pennsylvania v. Mimms. Unfortunately, this case law grants police officers the authority to order individuals to exit their vehicles during a lawful traffic stop. Cops do not have to fear for their safety in order to order you to step out of your vehicle as many people wrongly believe. I too had a misconception about this at one point. This shows the importance of continuous self-education.

Even if you conduct a flawless audit and have not violated any laws because of your thorough understanding of your state's laws, refusing to exit a vehicle during a lawful traffic stop can quickly turn your audit into a challenging situation. It's essential to be fully informed about what law enforcement can and cannot do to navigate such scenarios effectively.

Police Department Policies

Understanding the policies of the law enforcement agency in the jurisdiction where you are conducting an audit is of utmost importance. I've observed many auditors informing police officers about their obligation to identify to citizens, which is generally accurate. However, it's crucial to recognize that each policy may contain subtle variations, so you must be sure to quote the policy accurately. For instance, one policy might require an officer to identify him or herself to anyone they make contact with, while another may mandate identification to any member of the public whether the officer-initiated contact or not. Surprisingly, some policies may not address this matter at all.

Quoting the policy accurately sends a strong message to the officer, showing that you are knowledgeable, and you should be taken seriously. Misquoting the policy can give the impression that you're merely a disruptive YouTuber. Therefore, it is essential to thoroughly understand the officer's policy before claiming you have knowledge that you really do not possess. By doing this you won't find yourself with egg all over your face.

Effective Articulation Matters

Far too often we witness individuals struggling with the words 'Reasonable Articulable Suspicion.' Sometimes, the pronunciation is so poor that the police officer can't grasp what's being said—not because they're unaware of the concept, but it's due to the auditor struggling with the pronunciation.

To truly succeed when conducting an audit, you must be able to articulate with clarity and precision. Clarity is a major tool when challenging a police officer's Qualified Immunity. By making your words clear and stating the relevant laws to the police officer, you ensure they understand your point. Once you can demonstrate that the officer either clearly understood or willfully refused to understand, you initiate the process of taking away their Qualified Immunity.

Optimal Camera Coverage

Folks, it's absolutely crucial to ensure thorough camera coverage when recording interactions. Your goal should be to capture not only what the police officer is saying but also their body language and facial expressions. These non-verbal cues can be significant, especially when it comes to potential courtroom proceedings. Additionally, having a thorough recording makes it more convenient for you to review and analyze later.

Arrested or Not, Your Rights Can Be Violated

Here's a final tip worth sharing: YOU DO NOT NEED TO BE ARRESTED TO HAVE YOUR RIGHTS VIOLATED! Many individuals mistakenly believe that an arrest is a prerequisite for their rights to be infringed upon. Consequently, when they witness an auditor handing over his ID to a police officer under the threat of arrest, they often think the auditor have allowed their rights to be violated.

In truth, even if you are not formally arrested, your rights can still be violated the moment a police officer unlawfully forces you to do something without legal authority. This violation of your rights provides you with the grounds to file a complaint or pursue legal action, and if an arrest does occur, it can potentially strengthen your case if it was unlawful, but an arrest does not need to take place for your rights to be violated.

Auditing isn't going away any time soon unless, for some unusual reason, every police officer suddenly starts respecting the people's rights, and we all know that's unlikely to occur. If you're considering becoming an auditor, I urge you to do so with a genuine commitment to defending your rights and the rights of others. It should not be about getting clicks or possibly making money because, at that moment, no one truly benefits, and the fundamental purpose of auditing gets covered. Thank you for taking time to read this book. I sincerely hope it provided you with a pleasant and enriching experience.

God Bless!

About The Author

Abiyah Israel is a former law enforcement officer with a background that includes service in the United States Navy and Emergency Medical Services. He is originally from Boynton Beach, Florida.

His journey into law enforcement was motivated by not only a desire to obtain a career that he believed held prestige, but his experiences as a paramedic, where he witnessed firsthand the tragic consequences of child abuse. These experiences drove him to pursue a career in law enforcement with a determined mission to bring those responsible for harming children to justice. Mr. Israel dedicated himself to rigorous training and preparation, ultimately achieving excellence as a police officer and sheriff's deputy.

Throughout his law enforcement career, Mr. Israel confronted numerous challenges and harsh realities. Nevertheless, his commitment to sharing these experiences and insights with others remains steadfast. His goal is to educate and enlighten individuals about the intricate world of law enforcement and its profound impact on society.

Beyond his professional achievements, Mr. Israel takes pride in being a devoted husband and father to four children, including his eldest child, who is now 23 years old. His extensive life experiences, combined with his unique background, position him as an invaluable resource for those seeking a deeper understanding of the realm of law enforcement and its implications for our communities.

Abiyah Israel

For more information or to book interviews please contact

abiyah@wethepeopleuniversity.com

All rights reserved. Printed in the United States of America. No part of this book may be used or reproduced in any manner whatsoever without written permission except in the case of brief quotations em-bodied in critical articles or reviews.

Copyright © 2023 Abiyah Israel

All rights reserved.

Made in United States
Orlando, FL
07 May 2024